THE
GRAND PRL
DRIVERS
RACING HEROES FROM FANGIO TO PROST

THE
GRAND PRIX
DRIVERS

RACING HEROES FROM FANGIO TO PROST

EDITED BY STEVE SMALL

HAZLETON PUBLISHING, RICHMOND, SURREY

Publisher
RICHARD POULTER

Executive Publisher
ELIZABETH LE BRETON

Editor/Art Editor
STEVE SMALL

House Editor
S.G. SPARK

Publicity & Promotion
JANE PAYTON

Production
JANE DOYLE

Assistant
JOSS HOBBS

Cover photograph:
Niki Lauda.
by Paul-Henri Cahier

Title page:
The joy of victory:
1983 Canadian Grand Prix
winner René Arnoux (left)
is congratulated by
third-placed Ferrari team-mate
Patrick Tambay

Back cover photograph:
Alain Prost, champion again –
Adelaide 1986.
by King/SIPA Press

ACKNOWLEDGEMENTS

The Editor wishes to thank all the contributors and photographers for their enthusiasm and co-operation and particularly Maurice Hamilton for his invaluable assistance in the co-ordination of the project.

This first edition published in 1987 by Hazleton Publishing
3 Richmond Hill, Richmond, Surrey TW10 6RE.

ISBN: 0-905138-55-4

Printed in Great Britain by BAS Printers Ltd, Over Wallop, Hampshire.

Typeset by Solo Graphics, Twickenham, Middlesex.

DISTRIBUTORS

North America

Motorbooks International
PO Box 2
729 Prospect Ave.
Osceola
Wisconsin 54020
USA

Australia

Technical Book & Magazine Co. Pty Ltd
289-299 Swanston Street
Melbourne
Victoria 3000

New Zealand

David Bateman Ltd
PO Box 65062
Mairangi Bay
Auckland 10

UK & Other Markets

Osprey Publishing Ltd
12/14 Long Acre
London WC2E 9LP

INTRODUCTION

When the World Championship for Drivers was initiated in 1950, Giuseppe Farina won the British Grand Prix at Silverstone in a works Alfa Romeo at an average speed of 90.95 mph. Thirty-seven years later, Nigel Mansell triumphed at the same circuit in a Williams-Honda at an average speed of 146.208 mph.

The intervening years have seen startling technological advances in the design of the Grand Prix car as the sport continues its never-ending high-tech spiral. Amidst this 'progress' the one unchanging element is the human factor – the Grand Prix driver.

Great champions, personal favourites, boyhood heroes remain firmly in one's memory, but many are all but forgotten, reduced to mere statistics in the pages of motor racing history.

This book spotlights every outright Grand Prix winner since 1950. It is not, however, just a trip down memory lane. Journalistic and photographic talents combine in words and pictures to provide a unique insight into the men who have tasted victory at the sport's highest level.

Denis Jenkinson, Nigel Roebuck, Alan Henry and Maurice Hamilton have each concentrated on a decade of Grand Prix racing and, in their own highly personal way, assessed the drivers who starred in those eras. To avoid repetition, the drivers have generally been featured in the decade during which they were most successful, the only exceptions being three-time champions Brabham, Stewart and Lauda, whose achievements over many seasons insist upon further reflection.

Whilst the winners are the focus of this book, not forgotten are some of the most notable drivers, many of whom enjoyed illustrious careers and were distinctly unlucky not to have been rewarded with that elusive Grand Prix victory. They are featured at the end of each chapter.

It would be unfair to restrict our contributors by allowing them only to assess those drivers who fall into their particular decade. I have, therefore, invited them to attempt the near-impossible task of choosing their 'Top Ten' drivers from all four decades. In exercising their thoughts, they have reached some controversial conclusions which I am sure they will all agree are highly subjective – see if you concur!

Last, but certainly not least, a word of praise for the artistry of photographers Geoff Goddard, Nigel Snowdon and Diana Burnett. Their craft is highlighted in the outstanding photographs which play such a vital part in the book. In a single frame they consistently capture the personalities of the sportsmen in this elite group – the Grand Prix drivers.

Steve Small
Richmond, Surrey
July 1987

Black & White Photographs:
GEOFF GODDARD

Pages: 9-32, 34, 35, 37, 38, 40, 44, 46, 47, 48, 50, 53, 56,
61 *(centre left & below right)*, 62 *(below right)*, 63 *(centre right)*, 64,
96.

NIGEL SNOWDON

Pages: 3, 4-5, 33, 39, 41, 42, 43, 45, 49, 51, 52, 54, 55, 57, 58, 59, 60,
61 *(above right)*, 62 *(centre left & above right)*, 63, *(below left)*, 81-90,
92, 93, 94, 95, 100, 101, 102, 104, 105, 108, 109, 110,
111 *(above left, above right & below right)*,
112 *(centre left, centre right & below)*, 113, 114, 115, 120, 121, 122, 123,
124, 127, 132 *(below right)*, 133 *(below left)*,
134 *(above left & below left)*.

DIANA BURNETT

Pages: 63 *(above left)*, 91, 97, 98, 99, 103, 106, 107, 111 *(below left)*, 112
(above), 116, 117, 118, 119, 125, 128, 129, 130, 131,
132 *(centre left & above right)*, 133 *(above & centre right)*,
134 *(above & below right)*.

MARLBORO WORLD CHAMPIONSHIP TEAM

Page: 126.

LAT PHOTOGRAPHIC

Page: 36.

Colour Photographs:
GEOFF GODDARD

Pages: 65-71, 72 *(above)*, 73 *(above)*.

NIGEL SNOWDON

Pages: 72 *(below)*, 73 *(below)*, 74-80.

Froilan Gonzalez in the Ferrari defeats the
works Alfa Romeo team at the British Grand
Prix in 1951.

Known to his friends as 'Nino', Dr Farina had a long and successful career spanning the years 1934 to 1955, driving Alfa Romeo, Maserati and Ferrari cars as well as Tony Vandervell's Thinwall Special Ferrari. That Farina was a man of some substance, with a professional doctorate, was evident the moment you met him; he never really approved of workers, or *artisans,* becoming Grand Prix drivers, viewing the profession with a certain amount of pride and jealousy.

By 1937 Farina was a fully fledged member of the Alfa Romeo factory team run by the Scuderia Ferrari, but his skills did not reap their true reward as the Milanese cars were out-paced by the German Mercedes-Benz and Auto Union teams. None the less, Farina drove hard and fast. His driving was fearless and ruthless, and his character changed little when he was out of the cockpit (unlike some great drivers), although he could be charming and gracious when the occasion called for it. He was always master of his machinery, no matter what it was, but he was very hard on the mechanism – a car had to be strong to be driven by Farina. His 'laid-back' style, sitting well back from the steering wheel with arms at full stretch, had an almost regal air about it, in sharp contrast to most Grand Prix drivers of his day who tended to crouch over the wheel.

He won the last Grand Prix race to be held at Tripoli, driving a Tipo 158 Alfa Romeo, as Italy became embroiled in the European war in 1940. As soon as the war was over he reappeared with the Alfa Romeo factory team and was the pace-setter of the day. When Alfa Romeo withdrew for the 1949 season Farina drove for Ferrari and Maserati, and in 1950, when the FIA World Championship was introduced, Farina became the first official World Champion, winning the British GP, the Swiss GP and the Italian GP. Like many subsequent World Champions, he was not the best driver of his era when he won the title, but he was very competent at all times.

When Alfa Romeo finally withdrew in 1952, Farina joined the Scuderia Ferrari, but did not enjoy having to be number two to young Alberto Ascari. His innate pride was to be his downfall, for he became accident-prone through his inability to accept 'anno domini' and he could not ease up. In the 1954 Mille Miglia, when I came across the smoking wreck of Farina's 4.1 litre Ferrari smashed head-on into a tree soon after the start, it was no great surprise. He always managed to recover from his racing accidents and eventually retired in 1956, but died in a stupid road accident just ten years later.

The classic Farina style: on his way to victory at the
1950 British Grand Prix.

With such a famous father as Antonio Ascari, who was European Champion in 1925 driving for the Alfa Romeo team, young Alberto had a lot to live up to. Not only did he do this, but, in my estimation, he was the greatest Grand Prix driver of the 1950s. Perfection was his driving style, precise, accurate and unflustered. He seldom put a wheel wrong and his young team-mate in 1953, Mike Hawthorn, used to tell me what it was like to follow Ascari round a challenging circuit like Spa-Francorchamps. 'Bloody Ascari,' he would say, 'he is spot-on all the time and on every lap, there is never any variation.' This uncanny sense of judgement appeared everywhere in Ascari's driving, and never more so than at the start of a race. Photographs of starts in 1952 or 1953 invariably show a Ferrari way ahead on its own while most of the field are still controlling wheelspin. That will be Alberto Ascari.

Out of a racing car he was exactly the same: quiet and unruffled, nothing extrovert about his demeanour or behaviour; in fact, he was unobtrusive in the extreme. Being a racing driver was his chosen profession; it was not part of his family life, and he never encouraged his wife and family to accompany him, even to Monza, his local race track. This always struck me as strange, for Antonio had taken young Alberto to Monza when he was a small boy, as photos of him standing on the seat of an Alfa Romeo with his father on one side and Enzo Ferrari on the other, testify. If he didn't win a Grand Prix you could imagine Alberto returning to his home in Milan, opening the door, embracing his wife and children, and saying 'I've had a bad day at the office – what do we have for supper tonight?'

Not only was Alberto a devout Roman Catholic but he was inordinately superstitious, which used to amuse Fangio, who was practical and pragmatic. But that is the way Ascari was. He had a horror of black cats, and driving through a town he would turn round and take another route rather than pass a black cat sitting on the pavement.

It was while I was motoring across the South of France in the summer of 1955 that I heard with total disbelief on my car radio of his death at an unofficial test day at Monza. The undisputed King of Grand Prix racing in 1952 and 1953 was dead, and only a week after he had survived a plunge into the harbour in a Lancia D50 during the Monaco Grand Prix. As the car sank to the bottom of the harbour we all felt that Alberto would surely drown, but he bobbed up to the surface and swam strongly to the rescue boat. Yet now he had died in an unexplainable crash in a borrowed sports Ferrari.

Ascari was almost unbeatable with the T500 Ferrari.
Here he wins the 1953 Belgian Grand Prix at Spa.

If anyone had fire in his belly and a passion for racing it was the Argentinian 'Pepe' Gonzalez. His burly build and forceful, rather than elegant, driving style earned him the name 'Il Cabezon' (the Pampas Bull). Gonzalez in a Ferrari or Maserati was not a pretty sight to watch, but it was very exciting, and it seemed to matter little to him whether his car was on the track or on the grass verge . . . his foot was always hard on the accelerator pedal. He was a great friend of Fangio, but on the track they were real rivals.

'Pepe' came to Europe with Fangio in 1950 to race in the Argentine-sponsored Maserati team, but it was not long before he was invited to join the Scuderia Ferrari. His finest hour was at Silverstone in the 1951 British Grand Prix when, driving a 4½ litre V12 Ferrari, he beat the all-conquering Alfa Romeo 159 team. While no-one had fought harder against him than Fangio, equally no-one was more pleased at this victory than his fellow-countryman.

In 1955 he crashed in practice for the Tourist Trophy at Dundrod and although he raced again in his home country, for Europe the 'Pampas Bull' had been put out to grass.

I envy very few people in life, being well content with my own lifestyle, but one man I always envied was Piero Taruffi. A first class motor cyclist, a brilliant engineer, a competent Grand Prix driver, he was above all a man who knew how to live a full and interesting life, encompassing everything from engineering through music to the arts – a man who enjoyed travel, fine living, had excellent taste in all things and a controlled passion for motor racing. He was an accomplished linguist with an exceptional brain, able to deal with all aspects of life and to extract the best from everything. An engineer/racing driver of the best type.

I would have loved to have ridden with him in the Mille Miglia, for his knowledge of the 1000-mile route was quite remarkable. He had the ability to drive any sort of racing car, but the pureness of the Grand Prix car appealed to the engineer in him. Although not a World Champion racing driver, he was a true Grand Prix driver and a born perfectionist in all things.

In many people's eyes Juan Fangio was the greatest Grand Prix driver of all time; certainly, if results are how you judge greatness, then his record in Grand Prix racing will take some beating. Five times World Champion, using Alfa Romeo, Maserati, Mercedes-Benz and Ferrari cars, he won 24 of the 51 World Championship Grand Prix events which he contested. But Fangio was much more than a champion of statistics: he was a most likeable and friendly man, hard as nails in a Grand Prix car, yet gentle and *simpatico* out of the cockpit. He was shrewd when it came to business matters and had an uncanny foresight for choosing the teams for which he drove and the cars he used. However, he had his limitations as an all-round racing driver, showing little real interest in sports car racing, even though he drove in most of the big sports car events in the 1950s to fulfil contractual obligations.

He was born in Argentina in 1911 and raced in his own national events from 1934 to 1948, specialising in long-distance off-road marathons before turning to circuit racing with a home-made Chevrolet-engined single-seater. He made a brief foray to Europe in 1948, and in 1949 returned to make a full season of Grand Prix racing. He scored numerous victories and was so impressed that, despite his age (38), Alfa Romeo invited him to join their team of Tipo 158 'Alfettas'. With Alfa Romeo, his favourite make of racing car, he was World Champion in 1951, the first of his five championships.

He was admired and respected by all his contemporaries, especially the rising young stars who were quick to admit that 'the old man' was the greatest. If there was a fast corner that any of them could take nearly flat-out you could be sure that Fangio would take it absolutely flat-out. In later years when I asked him why he did things that the others could not or would not do, he replied simply: 'It was necessary; I was World Champion, and a true World Champion must always be the best'. He had the same philosophy about pole-positions.

He was 47 years old when he retired from Grand Prix racing and he left behind him a legend that those of us who saw it in the making will cherish for all time. It was a great honour to know this remarkable man, who still carries with him that uncanny air of 'World Champion' wherever he appears. Young racing drivers of today still feel deep emotion when they meet this Grand Old Man of Grand Prix. The name itself is enough: Fangio – a true master of the art of Grand Prix racing and one who is respected the world over.

The maestro: Fangio drifts the Maserati 250F
through a bend.

He was undoubtedly Britain's post-war wonder boy who could drive anything, anywhere at any time and always gave his maximum. He was a truly gifted artist at the wheel of a racing car who could even make bad cars look half-decent. He only knew one way to race and that was at 100 per cent; consequently his cars had to be strong, for if the car could give 100 per cent you knew that Stirling could use 110 per cent. It is doubtful whether any other driver has raced as great a variety of cars as he did, always excelling in whatever he drove. He worked 24 hours a day at being a professional racing driver for he reckoned that the paying public deserved to see him give of his best. Whether he was first or last he always put on a scintillating display of his skill and artistry.

He was one driver who was always ahead of his car's behaviour on the track, whereas others would be that fraction behind the car and its natural tendencies. Of the 66 World Championship Grand Prix races he contested he won 16, with 16 pole positions and 37 front row starts. His record in sports car racing was equally impressive, yet he was never crowned World Champion, and finished second four years in a row, three times behind Fangio and once behind Hawthorn.

If he had a fault it was his pride in being British, almost to the point of fanaticism; because of this he never joined the Scuderia Ferrari, who would have guaranteed him a World Championship. He got more pleasure out of racing for Rob Walker's private operation, a loner against the works teams, than he did in a factory team, even though he raced for HWM, Maserati, BRM and Vanwall. His exploits have filled many books, as have his escapes from racing accidents that were seldom his fault, but his career finally came to an end in 1962 with a crash at Goodwood.

He may not have been named a World Champion during his racing career from 1947 to 1962, but for me he was a World Champion driver, and the greatest all-rounder of his time. He was known in England as 'Mr Motor Racing', and justifiably so.

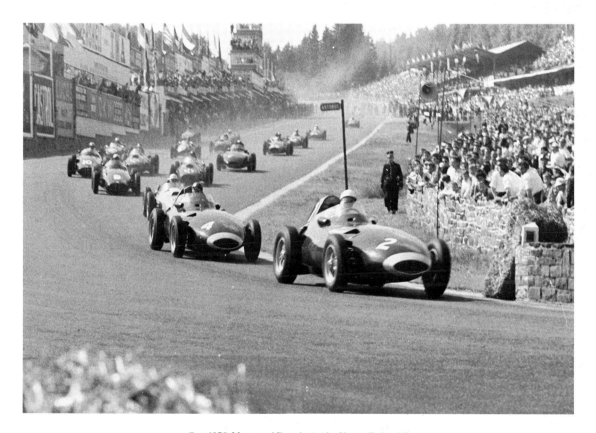

Spa 1958. Moss and Brooks in the Vanwalls lead the
field through Eau Rouge.

As British as the Royal Family and roast beef, Mike was a 'super bloke'. He was a motoring enthusiast at heart, having developed the taste for fast cars and racing from his father, Leslie. I am a bit biased about Mike Hawthorn as I lived only a few miles from his Farnham home, but he was one of the few drivers I enjoyed meeting in the local pub for a beer or two and a chin-wag. If I called in to his father's garage in Farnham with an interesting car or motor cycle, his first words would be 'let's have a go', and away he would go, to return windswept and beaming with pleasure.

He didn't have the natural talent of Stirling Moss or Tony Brooks, but he made up for it by sheer enthusiasm and bravery. If he took me for a ride around a circuit I used to think 'if I was brave enough, I could do what he is doing, but I know I don't have the bravery'. He could drive a sports car as well as he could drive a Grand Prix car, and one of his most memorable drives was in a D-type Jaguar in the Tourist Trophy at Dundrod in 1955. A Grand Prix that will remain in the memories of everyone who saw it was his battle against Fangio in 1953 at Reims, when he demonstrated clearly that a true-blue Englishman could take on the best and beat them. It was a great moment in Grand Prix history.

For many people, Mike's fetish for wearing a bow-tie while racing summed him up, but for me it was his 'flat 'at, pipe and pint of beer' when he wasn't racing that was the true Mike Hawthorn. His sense of fun at all times was natural and infectious. At one race, the prize-giving was upstairs in the town hall. We were all standing about in the foyer chatting when in came the fit and virile Stirling Moss, who bounded up the stairs two at a time and disappeared in a flash. Mike took the arm of his team-mate, Duncan Hamilton, and said 'Come on Duncan, we'd better join him', and in a splendid imitation of two very old men they helped each other up the stairs!

Mike's death in a road accident after he had retired from racing was tragic, but it was the result of his competitive spirit and willingness to 'have a go' at all times. I often think that Mike's last words before his Jaguar hit the tree must have been 'Oh F . . .'

Mike Hawthorn drives the Ferrari into third place at
the 1957 British Grand Prix, Aintree.

A product of the post-war 500 cc racing scene, Peter Collins soon demonstrated that he was capable of handling a lot more power than a motor cycle could provide. In quick leaps and bounds he was soon into serious racing, graduating from F2 HWM to the 400 horsepower of Mr Vandervell's Thinwall Special Ferrari. Aston Martin also gave him the opportunity to race in the long-distance classic races and inevitably he came to the notice of Ferrari, who took him into the Scuderia in 1956 with the Lancia-Ferrari V8 cars.

In the happy, carefree times of the 1950s a driver had the opportunity to race a large variety of cars in an equally varied choice of events, and Peter Collins did exactly that. He drove anything and everything, anywhere, thoroughly enjoying the casual life of the professional racing driver, even though his father's transport firm would have given him a steady job and good living.

He was not particularly popular with some team managers, as he had a tendency to 'lark about' if he felt the situation was not serious, but once in a racing car he settled down and drove in a hard and determined fashion, very similar in style to Mike Hawthorn, from whom he learnt a lot. Sadly, he crashed in the German GP at the Nürburgring in 1958, just in front of his chum Mike, and died shortly afterwards.

My lasting memory of Peter Collins was when I was on my way to the British Grand Prix at Aintree in my little Porsche 356. I drew up alongside a large articulated lorry at some traffic lights and realised the driver was hurling abuse down at me, the way lorry drivers can do. I looked up and there was Peter Collins grinning broadly from behind the wheel of the artic. He, too, was on his way to Aintree and was delivering the lorry for his father as it was on his route.

Peter Collins, a favoured 'son' of Ferrari. His gesture
in allowing Fangio to take his car at the 1956 Italian
Grand Prix will never be forgotten at Maranello.

The bearded Swede from the rich Stockholm family was not motivated by cars and racing so much as by the racing life, the travel, the good living and the international lifestyle. He was a very 'dry' character, with an aloof air and was not very outgoing. Although his English was near-perfect it did have that slightly Scandinavian ring to it, but he always spoke slowly and quietly, seldom showing any emotion, even under stress.

He won only one Grand Prix race, despite taking part in more than a hundred, always driving for factory teams after his first two seasons with his own Maserati. His victory came with BRM in the 1959 Dutch Grand Prix at Zandvoort, and I am sure he was as surprised about it as anyone.

Whereas the rough and ready racing characters like Fangio or Hawthorn never gave safety a first thought, let alone a second, drivers like Bonnier were more interested in living than in winning. It was ironic that his death at Le Mans came because the safety barriers were not high enough to stop his little Lola flying over them and into the trees.

When I first saw Tony Brooks in action, he stood out head and shoulders above everyone else – not by reason of winning races, but by his poise and style of driving. The car was right on the limit of tyre adhesion, yet perfectly balanced and smooth, with the driver showing no signs of working hard or juggling with the situation. Clearly here was a man with a delicate touch, a fine sense of balance and a natural flair for speed. Tony's driving style complemented the evolution in racing car design. Being of slight build, he drove with his brain and his finger tips, rather than his arm muscles and a big heart. None the less, his passion for racing was all-absorbing.

I was lucky enough to be at the 1955 Syracuse Grand Prix when Tony trounced the works Maserati team, driving a Connaught. He did it in such an effortless manner that the organisers felt forced to have the Connaught engine dismantled to make sure it was not over the limit of 2½ litres. At that point few people had heard of Tony Brooks, but that all changed, for his association with the Vanwall team and later with the Scuderia Ferrari put Tony Brooks near the top of the Grand Prix tree.

The Cooper Years

The nut-brown Brabham from Sydney, Australia, was the perfect example of a garage mechanic turned Grand Prix driver. He was not an engineer in the academic sense, but he was a gifted fettler and he knew exactly what he wanted of a racing car, even if others disagreed. He came to the European scene in the mid-1950s, knocking on people's doors to see if they wanted a racing driver. John Cooper, of Cooper Cars, decided he wanted one and a partnership started which culminated in Jack Brabham and Cooper winning the Formula 1 World Championship in 1959 and 1960.

He was a shrewd businessman and was the inspiration behind Cooper Cars' racing efforts. What Jack wanted Cooper gave him, with very satisfying results. I well recall talking to John Cooper one winter and asking about his Formula 1 car for the next season. He said, with all honesty, 'I can't tell you until Jack gets back from Australia'.

Jack's actual driving talent was nothing very special, but his knowledge of racing and track-craft was hard to beat. Coupled with his business sense, Jack's racing was very successful in more than results on paper. People would say that he would only really start going when he heard the cash-register beginning to ring up the winnings – and they were not far wrong.

His ability to tune an engine and set up the chassis for what he wanted from the car was a natural gift and I had a long technical discussion with him one day when Cooper were just getting into Formula 1. He described to me in great detail just what he was aiming to achieve in the way of steering and handling, even though he could not explain the theory, and I found it fascinating to listen to him. Three years earlier I had had a similar discussion with the Daimler-Benz engineers on racing car design, except that they were explaining it to me mathematically. The end result of the two discussions was the same!

The real worth of Jack Brabham's stature in Grand Prix racing can be judged by the pleasure with which everyone sees him today when he turns up at a Grand Prix to see how things are going. One characteristic he has never lost is his use of one word in answer to a question when the questioner was hoping for a whole sentence! Taciturn, I think they call it.

Halcyon days, when Brabham and Cooper were a
dominant force in the 2½ litre formula.

Maurice grew up amid racing and he was soon taking part in minor French events. When war broke out he stored his Bugatti in a barn in the family vineyards where, unknown to him, rats nested in the fuel tank. Once peace had returned, Maurice retrieved the car and entered for the first race in France in 1945. He retired with fuel lines choked by *petoulet*, the French slang for 'rat shit', which became his nickname. In fact, it was a real contradiction for he was always neat and immaculate, and he drove in the same way.

In the post-war years 'Petoulet' was one of the 'Three Musketeers', the trio of French drivers who did so much for the little Gordini team that strove valiantly to uphold French honour in Grand Prix racing. By 1954 Maurice had earned his way into the Ferrari works team, and later drove Rob Walker's Cooper-Climax. He stayed in Grand Prix racing a little too long, ending his career in 1964 in a private BRM team of not very high standards. However, in France he will always be remembered for the way he drove 'pour la patrie'.

HARRY SCHELL:
Playboy –
the original
American
in Paris.

JEAN BEHRA:
Tiger.

LUIGI VILLORESI: Grand old man.

LUIGI FAGLIOLI: Pre-war ace.

LUIGI MUSSO:
Very proud of Italy.

EUGENIO CASTELLOTTI:
Very proud of being an Italian.

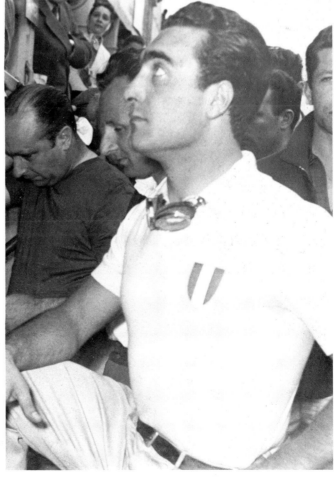

ROY SALVADORI: Aerodrome racer.

STUART LEWIS-EVANS *(centre):* A new era;
brain before brawn.

Jochen Rindt in the Cooper-Maserati dives
inside the Ferrari of Chris Amon at La Source
hairpin, 1967 Belgian Grand Prix.

Given his time over again, Phil Hill says he would never be a racing driver. And to suggest that a career second time around could work out so well is probably stretching credibility too far. In nearly 20 years of racing, Hill won the World Championship, the Le Mans 24 Hours three times, as well as countless other races – and never once was he hurt. No-one can reasonably ask more than that.

Phil, in fact, was a racing driver in spite of himself. Introspective and edgy before a race, he would pace up and down, lighting one cigarette after another, like a man on Death Row. But once in the car, once under way, the nerves calmed, doubts disappeared; his style became easy and composed. He was one of those, like Brooks or Rodriguez or Ickx, who excelled at the unyielding circuits. And he shone, too, in treacherous conditions.

For years the quiet Californian had his sights on Formula 1, but Enzo Ferrari considered him a sports car driver. Only when Musso and Collins were killed within a month of each other, in the summer of 1958, was Phil brought in to partner Hawthorn at Monza. In a sensational debut, he led much of the way, and his Grand Prix future was assured.

Perhaps he was at his greatest in 1960, when Ferrari – still front-engined – were outclassed on all but the very fastest circuits. In the beautiful Dino 246 Phil took a miraculous third at Monaco, pressured Brabham hard at Spa, shone at Oporto, finally won at Monza.

Hill's time truly came the following year, when only he and Ferrari teammate von Trips were in serious contention for the World Championship. And Phil clinched the title at Monza in the most sorrowful circumstances imaginable. Taffy had been killed early in the race, and on the rostrum the face of America's first World Champion was drawn, eyes glazed.

Perhaps he should have retired at that point. Certainly his friends thought so. But Hill was firmly wedded to his way of life by now, had grown accustomed to the ways of Italy, where he could indulge his passion for music, go to La Scala in Milan whenever he chose.

It is doubtful that anyone more intelligent than this gentle and perceptive man has ever sat in a racing car. At the end of 1967 he felt that enough was enough, slipped back to the West Coast, got married, relaxed at last.

Phil Hill's 1961 World Championship was the
pinnacle of his career, though he will be
remembered by many as one of sports car racing's
greatest drivers.

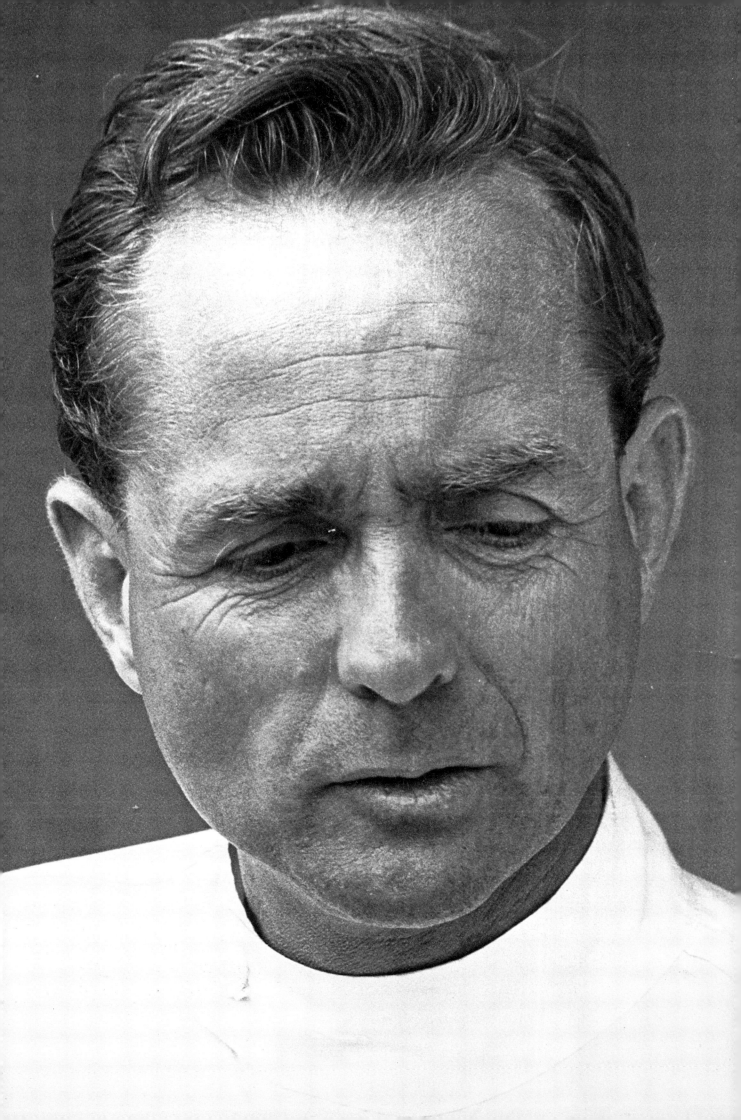

Count von Trips was a gentleman in the real sense of the word, and he raced cars because he had a passion for it. Ferrari loved him for his courteous manners and humour, and also for his utter fearlessness. The Old Man's favourites have always been abnormally brave.

For most of his career von Trips was confined largely to sports car racing. Occasional Formula 1 drives left no doubts that he was quick enough, but there were several huge accidents, and it was not until 1960 that Ferrari gave him a permanent place in the Grand Prix team.

All he knew about cars was how to drive them, and in those days that was how they liked their drivers at Maranello. 'Leave the technical stuff to us' was their maxim, and Taffy was only too happy to comply.

In 1961 the Ferrari 156, with classic 'sharknose' profile, was the thing to have, and at last it all looked to be coming right for von Trips. He won at Zandvoort, took another fine victory at Aintree in the rain, scored well everywhere. Leading the World Championship from team-mate Phil Hill, he went to Monza, took pole position. And on the second lap, after a touch with Clark, he went off the road and was killed instantly.

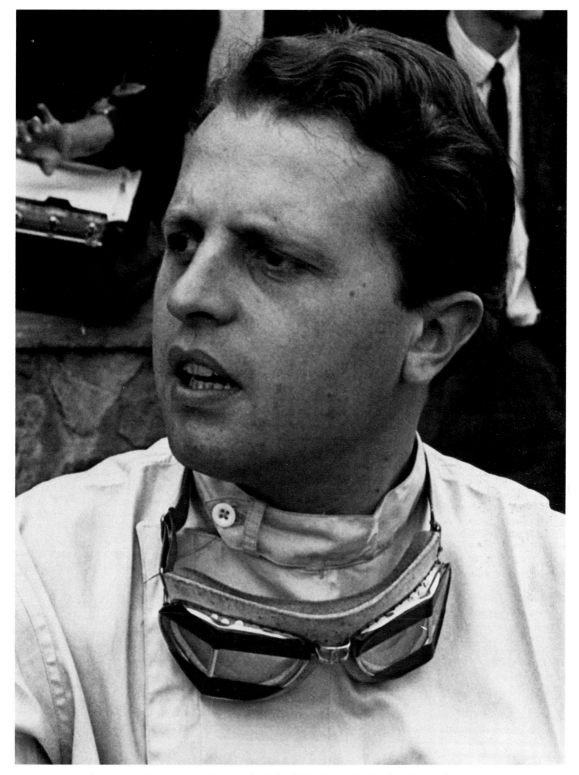

On a wet afternoon at Aintree, in July 1961, Giancarlo Baghetti's sharknose Ferrari spun and slid off the road, hitting a fence. An extraordinary sequence of events had come to an end. The Italian had come to the British Grand Prix with an unbeaten record: three races, three wins.

Baghetti's Grand Prix career, although brief, was remarkable. In March 1961 he drove a Ferrari in his first Formula 1 race, at Siracusa, and won it, after a battle with Gurney's Porsche. Two months later came his second event, in Naples, and that that he also took. Finally, in July, he took part in his first Grande Epreuve, the French Grand Prix at Reims. And, astoundingly, that race, too, ended in dramatic victory for him – again over Gurney.

That, though, was the long and short of it. Afterwards Giancarlo never did anything worth a damn in Formula 1. He had a full season with Ferrari in '62, moved to the calamitous ATS team the following year, and after that took rides as and when they cropped up. A sort of lesser Scarfiotti, he was a charming fellow, of considerable wealth, who slipped out of racing quietly. It had been, in effect, a career in reverse.

Richie Ginther was the perfect second driver. Although he had great days in his F1 career, he was never consistently on a par with Clark, Hill or Gurney. He knew it and accepted it, as honest with himself as with others.

For all that, he was more than a journeyman and this tiny Californian was rarely far off the absolute pace. While leading the 1961 French Grand Prix at Reims, he felt the engine beginning to tighten up, and so he came in, parked the car, walked away. The Ferrari mechanics could not believe it, but that was Ginther: he hated to abuse machinery.

This extraordinary mechanical sympathy, quite untypical of the era, made him a fine test driver and he was used to great effect by Ferrari and BRM. When Honda got serious about Formula 1, in 1965, Richie was the perfect choice to lead the team and he won with the Japanese car in Mexico – the last race of the 1500 cc Formula 1.

In 1967 he briefly partnered Gurney in the Eagle-Weslakes, then, quite out of the blue, told Dan he wanted to stop. Simply, he felt the time was right, and he never drove a race car again.

Ireland was born ten years too late. With his attitude to racing he should have been a Grand Prix driver through the Fifties, a colleague of Collins, Hawthorn and Schell. His style belonged in a Maserati 250F. As it was, he arrived at a time of transition, when engines were moving behind the driver, when drivers were spending less time behind the bar.

After occasional Lotus drives in 1959, Ireland fairly burst upon the GP scene early in 1960, winning at both Goodwood and Silverstone in Chapman's rear-engined 18. Later that year, he led Moss and Brabham at Oulton Park, went off the road and repassed them within a few laps.

Innes was very quick, had a lot of accidents over the years, and was always prepared to run at the limit. His last-lap victory over the Porsches at Solitude in 1961 was unforgettable. Later the same year, at Watkins Glen, he scored Team Lotus's first Grand Prix victory, but soon afterwards Chapman decided that Ireland no longer figured in his plans. It was too late to find another competitive ride, and sadly Innes never again drove for a top team.

After Clark's death, in early 1968, Chris Amon eloquently summed up the feelings of the drivers: 'Beyond the grief, there was also a fear which we all felt. If it could happen to him, what chance did the rest of us have? It seemed we'd lost our leader . . .'

After Moss's enforced retirement in 1962, Jim swiftly and quite naturally took over as the yardstick by which others were judged, and perhaps no racing driver in history has dominated an era quite as he did. It may be argued that racing was less competitive in his time than now, and certainly the Lotus was usually the best car. But beyond dispute, too, is that he was by a league the best of his time – perhaps the best of any time.

Consider the bare statistics of those eight Formula 1 seasons: 25 wins, 33 pole positions, 27 fastest laps . . . and all from 72 starts. But the single fact which tells most about Clark is that only once did he finish second. In other words, if he made it to the flag, he invariably made it before anyone else.

It seems inappropriate that history tends to shackle Jim's memory to the 1.5 litre era, for these were hardly Grand Prix cars for the Gods. And the truth is that, whatever the regulations of his time, the quietly-spoken Scot would have ruled. He had it all.

Clark's entire character changed when he got into a racing car. Outside it, he was a nervous man for most of his life. Only in his last years did he come to realise, and accept, his status, becoming more confident and worldly. But he never stopped biting his nails, and he shrank from making speeches.

Usually he was courteous, kind, wry. And his pure love of motor racing was beyond question; money was always a secondary consideration. He would have detested the sport as it is today, with commercialism rampant, PR persons at every turn. Jim Clark was a man of action, not words. A man to whom races seemed to surrender, one who, like Ascari, won by imperious command. A man who, in 1967, took pole position at the Nürburgring by *nine* seconds and more.

That was his last full season, and we saw him at his greatest, which was very great indeed. No mannerly Lotus 25, this. It was the 49, with prototype Cosworth DFV engine, a wayward package which had to be fought. Four times he won with it that year, and another in his last Grand Prix, at Kyalami early in 1968, brought the tally up to 25. Without that tyre failure at grey and rainy Hockenheim on 7 April, who knows what kind of figure Alain Prost might now be shooting for? Jim was 32 and at his zenith.

In the hands of Jim Clark the Lotus 49 was
uncatchable. He led every Grand Prix for which
they were entered and only unreliability denied him
the 1967 World Championship.

'He's a Graham Hill', has become over the years a Formula 1 catchphrase to describe any driver whose success apparently owes more to guts and determination than to natural ability. During the Sixties Clark and Gurney were regarded as the naturals, Hill the worker who got there by application and sweat. And Graham would bristle at that.

It was, of course, all relative. No man entirely devoid of raw talent could have won the World Championship (twice), the Indianapolis 500 and the Le Mans 24 Hours. And what of five victories in the Monaco Grand Prix?

Some might argue that Graham's need to work, to practise, to calculate, makes his success the more admirable. With no family wealth to support him, he worked his passage into motor racing, trading his services as a mechanic for the odd drive. It was this tactic which got him into Team Lotus.

The meat of Hill's career, though, was spent at BRM, 10 of his 14 Grand Prix victories being won between 1962 and 1965. After seven years there he returned to Lotus, and the real quality of the man was never more apparent than in 1968, following the death of Clark.

Jimmy had *been* Team Lotus, yet somehow, in the dreadful aftermath of Hockenheim, Graham kept Chapman and his men together, strengthened their resolve, made them start again. At Járama, the first race without Clark, Hill won. Then came Monte Carlo, and he won there, too. At 39, he was telling them that he was ready to be World Champion again.

After his huge accident at Watkins Glen in 1969, in which he severely injured his legs, many would have been happy to see Graham quit. He was 40, and had done it all. But retiring in those circumstances was not the man's way. There was something to conquer here, and so he conquered it. He even won again, at the International Trophy in 1971 for Brabham, and at Le Mans the following year for Matra.

In 1973 he formed his own team, and his last two seasons were a sad embarrassment to all who had seen him at his peak. Especially poignant was the sight of him climbing from his car at Monaco in 1975, having failed to qualify for this, the race he had made his own. He never drove again.

When he died, along with members of his team, that freezing November night, there was enormous grief at the news. Graham was held in affection by people who had never been near a race circuit. His personality and humour had taken him beyond his own immediate sphere. And now a national institution had been lost.

After the loss of Clark at Hockenheim Graham Hill
rallied the Lotus team round with victories at
Járama and Monaco *(above)*. This second World
Championship in 1968 was universally popular.

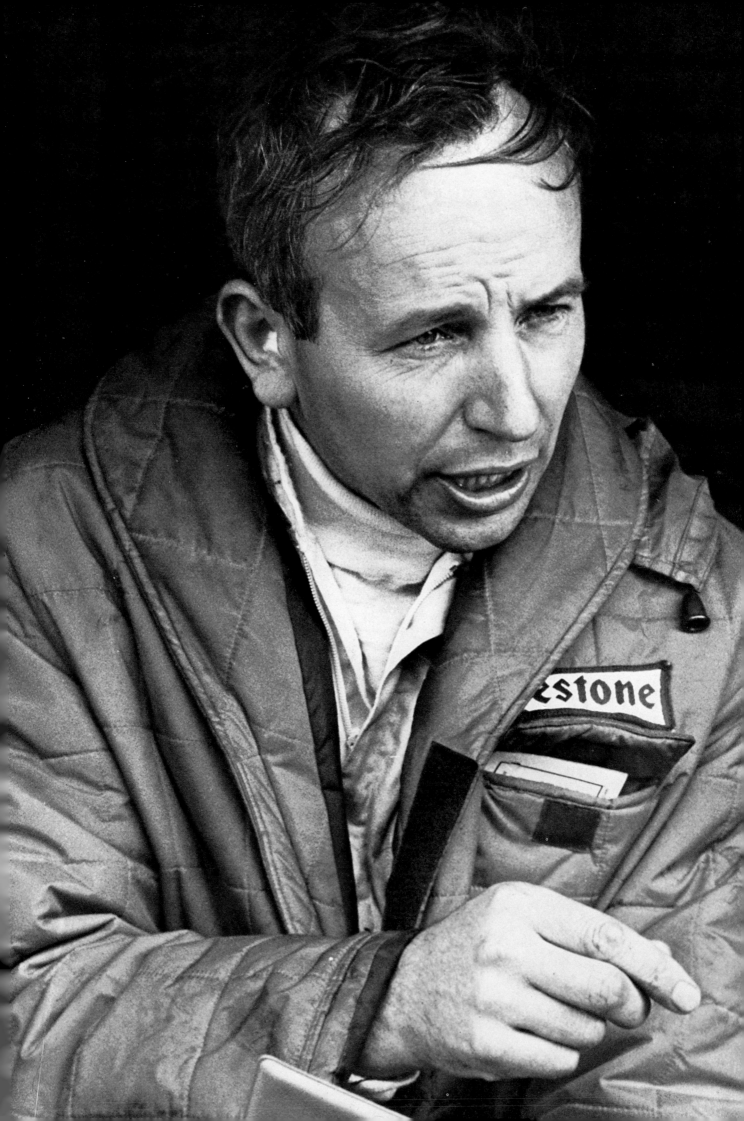

The tragedy of John Surtees is that people tend to remember him as the Formula 1 constructor who failed, who left the sport a disillusioned man. Often overlooked is his greatness as a racing driver.

And he *was* great. The transition from bikes to cars was made with barely a break in stride. In June of 1960 he dominated TT week on the MV Agusta, and the following month drove a Lotus to second place in the British Grand Prix. By mid-August, in Portugal, he had the car on pole position and ran away with the race until retirement. Other Lotus drivers at Oporto included Moss and Clark . . .

The Ferrari years produced one World Championship, in 1964, and there would surely have been a second, two years later, had not driver and team split at mid-season.

Throughout his career Surtees never learned diplomacy, which is another way of saying that old-fashioned qualities like adherence to principle still counted with him. He always spoke his mind, a quality scarcely universal in Grand Prix racing, and sometimes he did it witheringly. In truth, he never fitted in as comfortably as he had in the less 'precious' motor cycle world.

Two years with Honda brought out the best and worst in John. His dedication to the project was unflagging, and many times he had the heavy and wilful V12 into places it had no business to be. At Monza in 1967 he even won with it. But the enthusiasm was ground away by frustration with the slow-moving Japanese. It was a partnership which should have produced more.

A season with BRM, in 1969, was worse, far worse, to the point that he can hardly bring himself to discuss it even today. After that he decided to follow the example of Brabham and McLaren, to form his own team. At the end of 1971 he retired as a driver.

Had Surtees been content merely to drive, who knows what he might have achieved? Although he would often stress that he was not an engineer, too often he tried to behave like one. This, wherever he went, caused friction, and inevitably took a toll of his driving. No-one can do it all.

At his best, John was a racer of the purest kind, a driver of deftness and enormous courage, exactly the fellow to shine at Spa in the wet. In hindsight he seems invariably to have chosen the difficult route. But he probably wouldn't agree . . .

A superb photograph of Surtees and the Honda on
the limit at the 1967 British Grand Prix.

For Lorenzo Bandini, Grand Prix racing *was* Ferrari. The notion of driving for anyone else would have been inconceivable, and there can be little doubt that he raced at least as much for the old man of Maranello as for himself. Through his years of childhood poverty, he had dreamed only of becoming a Ferrari driver.

The sadness was that Lorenzo never made it to the summit. He was a fine driver, sometimes a brilliant one, but never great. Only in the last few months of his life were there signs of fully realising all that early potential.

He won only once, at Zeltweg in 1964, but there should have been more. For most of his career at Ferrari, he was a loyal number two to Surtees, but for 1967 was finally and unequivocally *numero uno*. At Monte Carlo he qualified on the front row, led at the start, and in the late stages was chasing Hulme when he crashed appallingly at the chicane. Terribly burned, he died three days later. Bandini's accident, seen on television screens across the world, had a massive effect on the future of racing safety, but that was of little consolation in Italy, which mourned the loss of a favourite son.

Scarfiotti is one of those anomalies who must inevitably find their way into a book of this kind. It is ironic that Chris Amon, one of his Ferrari team-mates in the Sixties, and an incomparably greater driver, is absent because somehow he never did win a Grand Prix. But 'Lulu' did, and it came at the best possible place – Monza. The 1966 Italian was one of only ten Grands Prix in which he competed.

Grandson of the first president of Fiat, cousin of Gianni Agnelli, Scarfiotti was born into extraordinary wealth. His life could have been one of carelessness and ease, and it was perhaps this which drove him to seek a means of testing himself. A man of humour and debonair charm, he developed into a magnificent sports car driver, but the dream was always Formula 1.

Ferrari, though, believed it beyond Scarfiotti. Despite the impressive Monza victory, there were only a couple of drives afterwards. Ludovico, assuredly the last of the true gentlemen racers, signed Cooper and Porsche contracts for 1968, and it was in one of the German sports cars that he lost his life, practising at the Rossfeld hill climb in June.

Dan Gurney never won the World Championship, nor even came close. Yet he was the rival most truly feared by Clark, and it seems barely credible that the man who was perhaps the greatest American Grand Prix driver ever took only four victories from all those years.

The classic circuits always drew out the best in him, and perhaps Spa-Francorchamps was his favourite. In 1964 he and the Brabham were in their own class there, on the pole and in front all the way until the last lap, when the fuel ran out. Fittingly, though, Gurney's only Grand Prix win in his own gorgeous Eagle-Weslake came at Spa three years later.

There were those who claimed Dan to be hard on his cars, and it is undeniable that he was known actually to have broken the gear lever, even the steering wheel, in the course of a race. But his style in the race car was as relaxed as his manner out of it. A delightful man, he never got bitter, never lost his humour or zest, however frequently his cards came from the bottom of the pack. He had a feel for the roots of motor racing; you watched his face during a demonstration by Fangio and you saw a schoolboy's enthusiasm, untouched by the hostile Fates.

McLaren was never going to die in a racing car, just as Nuvolari would never live to retire. Yet the Italian succumbed to tuberculosis at 61, and Bruce was killed in a freak accident, testing at Goodwood on a Tuesday afternoon.

As a Formula 1 driver, he is difficult to place. More than a mere journeyman, he was never in the first rank. You looked to McLaren to take thirds and fourths, to score points consistently. Yet when the mood took him – as at the Race of Champions in 1968 – he could be devastating, and he remains the youngest man ever to win a Grand Prix. He was just 22 when he took the flag at Sebring in late 1959.

A modest and friendly man, Bruce seemed to carry his personality with him into a Grand Prix race: winning was not *that* important. You rarely saw him truly chance his arm. When his own F1 team got properly under way, in '68, he was quite content to play second driver to Hulme.

You sensed, too, that retirement was not far away. The future was McLaren Cars. The company: that was what brought his real ambition into play. As a driver, Bruce never had the ego so essential to stars; long-term what he wanted was to direct.

JACK BRABHAM

The Brabham Years

In Europe Brabham was never a man to capture the public imagination. Quiet and undemonstrative, he never used two words where one would do, never became 'worldly'. Travelling constantly brought its own problems, and he would take steaks out from England with him, wary of the effects of foreign food. He was one of the first drivers to fly to races in his own aeroplane, and it must amuse him that now it is *de rigueur* among the fashionable. Jack kept to himself. It was no matter of being unfriendly; simply, he was an introvert.

On the track, though, it was a different matter. There was nothing shy about Jack Brabham, racing driver. His apprenticeship, served on the dirt ovals of New South Wales, had been rough and tumble, and Black Jack knew every trick in the book. Some said he wrote the book. Time and again one of his rear wheels would edge off the road, pepper those behind with gravel and dirt. He came of a hard school, and accepted the knocks as he handed them out. And at the end of the race there was inevitably that innocent flicker of a smile. Who, me?

Brabham was a doughty competitor. His style – shoulders hunched, head down – was never elegant, but in full cry he was a mighty impressive sight.

As he pioneered private flying among the drivers, so Jack was also the first to form his own team. The early Cooper years had been wonderful, bringing back-to-back World Championships, but later his horizons changed, and the first F1 Brabham appeared at the German Grand Prix in 1962.

For the next three seasons he was happy enough to be number two, in his own team, to Dan Gurney. But in 1966 Jack began a memorable Indian summer. In this, the first year of the new 3 litre Formula 1, the team's Repco engines were not to the forefront on horsepower, but what they had they gave for ever. At Reims, nearly six years after his last victory, Brabham became the first man to win a Grand Prix in a car bearing his own name. He also took the next three races – and his third title.

To the end of his career, Jack was always a factor. In his final season, 1970, he had one win and should have had several more. In Mexico, his last race, the Ferraris were beyond reach, but when he retired Brabham was running third. At 44, he was still in there, still pitching.

Brabham at the 1966 German Grand Prix

Denis Clive Hulme is one of history's more unlikely World Champions. Surely no-one that laid back could have made it to the pinnacle? But Denny did.

He is, by his own admission, a lazy fellow, his entire approach to life always a matter of taking the simplest, most direct route. Denny disliked uncertainties, making a point, for example of staying in Holiday Inns whenever possible. Buenos Aires or Berlin, they were all exactly the same, and that was what he liked about them.

Similarly, Hulme liked to have everything weighed up on the race track. Like Scheckter, he never saw Formula 1 remotely as a romantic thing. Paramount in both their minds was survival: if it were wet during practice, very well, Denny sat the session out. After all, the rain always stopped eventually, didn't it?

In the quest to improve safety in Grand Prix racing, the New Zealander contributed more than anyone save Stewart. Behind the gruff and sometimes intimidating public face there was a sensitive man, deeply affected by tragedy in the sport. It was the manner of Peter Revson's death, in 1974, which determined Denny to quit once and for all.

This sells short his career, however. You could have got spectacular odds on Hulme for the World Championship in 1967. With but a season and a bit of Formula 1 behind him, he and the Brabham scarcely looked a serious rival for Clark, Hill and so on. True enough, he won only twice that year, but they were prestigious victories, at Monte Carlo and the Nürburgring. And, when they added up the points, he had more than anyone else.

It was typical of Denny that by then he had already decided to change teams; Bruce McLaren was mounting a serious Formula 1 effort for 1968. Hulme liked the look of it, and Bruce was a friend. QED, mate.

To the end of his career, Denny remained a McLaren driver. Perhaps he coasted through his final season, but until then he was never to be discounted. Once in a while, as at Kyalami in 1971, he was simply the fastest man in the place. And when victory was a real possibility, Hulme could, and would, race with anyone. During the closing laps at Anderstorp in 1973 he switched off the rev limiter, got his head down and passed the ailing Peterson with a couple of laps to go.

And it all ended quietly, just as he would have wished. Four laps into the US Grand Prix of 1974 Denny's engine blew. Yes, he smilingly said, that was it, finish. Now it was back to New Zealand, health and humour intact.

Denny Hulme; a greatly underrated driver who shone in all types of racing. His World Championship in 1967 was with Brabham, but he moved on to become a key figure in the McLaren team.

Jochen Rindt . . . what do we remember of him? The mesmeric car control, the deep, clipped voice, the boxer's nose, tousled hair. And we who saw him, perhaps we recall the swell of sound from the grandstands which greeted his approach on one of the great days.

In every era there should be someone like Jochen, someone to bring a race to life, make it crackle. Ronnie was another such, Gilles perhaps the most extreme example of all. Each won races in cars which had no business winning races. It rarely happens, but when it does, the day inevitably passes into legend.

Rindt's early career gave no hint of the greatness to come. As a Formula Junior driver in the early Sixties he was remarkable only for flamboyant dress and a loud mouth, but once into Formula 2 he swiftly asserted himself. In Grand Prix racing, though, three seasons with Cooper and one with Brabham yielded little. Jochen's Formula 1 career began to flourish only when he joined Lotus in 1969.

It was a year of highs and lows. The Austrian quickly established himself as Stewart's only serious rival, but through most of the season Lotus reliability was wretched. Colin Chapman, fearful of losing Jochen, spoke of the revolutionary car he had planned for 1970, promised him absolute priority within the team. Rindt was persuaded, and at Watkins Glen finally won his first Grand Prix. It had been no better than any of his drives that year, he said. For once the car had stayed together.

As Chapman had promised, the new Lotus 72 made everything else obsolete. In 1970 Jochen won consecutively at Zandvoort, Clermont Ferrand, Brands Hatch and Hockenheim. Before these, however, had come a win at Monaco in the old 49, and this was Rindt's day of days. Even now, these many years later, people stand in Casino Square and recall that May afternoon. For Jochen the merest scent of victory was enough, and in the closing laps he showed them genius as he chased Brabham.

Often arrogant and intolerant of fools, he wasn't for everyone. Yet he had about him, too, a vulnerability. Through that last summer he worried that suddenly everything was going almost too well for him. The others were having the bad luck; the title was as good as won.

He lost his life during the final qualifying session at Monza, when 'something broke' on the Lotus 72. He is recorded in the history books as the only posthumous World Champion. Those who saw him, though, remember Jochen chiefly for this: he made them catch their breath.

Rindt in typical shape with the Lotus 72, a car which
at last allowed him to fulfil his potential but in
which he was tragically to lose his life.

Think of Seppi, and you remember first a fearlessness that could be chilling. You watched him, and often you feared for him; there was a streak of wildness there, and the limits seemed fuzzy, ill-defined.

A gentle fellow, with a fine sense of humour, Siffert was popular with the other drivers, but some were wary of him during working hours, running wheel to wheel at, say, Monza. In these circumstances, Stewart would say, Seppi rather tended to live for the moment.

He was never a polished Grand Prix driver, in the Lauda sense of the word, never one to give his cars an easy time. Often he was over kerbs, brushing banks, sideways. There were others of greater natural gift, who perhaps needed to give less of themselves, but after every race in which he drove, you knew that Siffert had been at the limit. That was the man. His background was the poorest of the poor, but his love of racing, his commitment to it, took him finally into Formula 1.

We remember Siffert chiefly for his days in the Rob Walker Lotus 49, but in 1971 he joined BRM, heroically taking over the team leadership after the death of Rodriguez. Only three months later Seppi, too, was gone.

He was a fatalist, Pedro, a man who believed absolutely that God called the shots. His philosophy was always evident in his driving, at once stylish and fearless. Rodriguez, child of arid Mexico, was never better than in treacherous and uncertain conditions.

Driving sports cars for John Wyer, and with BRM in Formula 1, Pedro settled happily in England. When he arrived at a circuit, it was in a sedately driven Bentley, and on his swept-back black hair sat a Bond Street deerstalker. But once into overalls, there was no hint of the dilettante. No-one raced harder than Rodriguez, and his stamina was a legend.

Spa-Francorchamps (the old circuit, of course) brought out every great quality in him. Amon, who tailed him throughout the Belgian Grand Prix of 1970, reported that his precision through the fast sweepers was absolute. Through history Pedro's name will be synonymous with the Porsche 917, but this day in the V12 BRM was his greatest.

It was his passion for the sport which killed him. A weekend without a race was a weekend lost, so he accepted an Interserie sports car drive at the Norisring in July 1971. And there he died by someone else's error.

The Sixties

The most immediately evident feature of Jackie Stewart was his confidence. It was in everything he did, and right from the beginning. After a stunning F3 season with Ken Tyrrell in 1964, he had the choice of Lotus or BRM – the blue riband rides of the time – for his Formula 1 debut the following year. And here came early signs of a man who knew precisely where he was going.

Most attractive on paper had to be the Lotus drive. It was the fastest car in Grand Prix racing, and would have made Stewart team-mate to Jim Clark, a man he revered. But Jackie considered: this was a team which quite properly concentrated its energies on Clark. The number two Lotus, by legend, rarely made the finish. As well as that, Colin Chapman was a man who demanded results – and quickly. Better, Stewart reasoned, to do without that kind of pressure in his first season, to accept a sound, competitive car from BRM, learn from team leader Graham Hill and play himself in.

It was the right course to follow. After only a few races he had the measure of Hill, and swiftly emerged as the natural rival to Clark. At Monza he took the first of his 27 Grand Prix victories.

In 1966 he began with a top-drawer win in Monte Carlo, but at Spa came an accident he was fortunate to survive. It was to change fundamentally and for ever racing's traditionally *laissez-faire* attitude to safety. Trapped in the inverted car for several minutes, Stewart was soaked in fuel. He had a long time to be frightened, and thereafter cared not whom he upset: he was going to make racing as safe as it could reasonably be. Every Grand Prix driver of the last twenty years is in his debt.

After Clark's death, in early 1968, Jackie took over as The Man. Driving a Matra-Cosworth for Ken Tyrrell, he won three times that year, including that unforgettable day in the rain and drear at the Nürburgring. Second man Hill was more than four minutes behind . . .

There were six wins in 1969, easily enough to carry JYS to his first World Championship at the wheel of the Matra MS80, which stands to this day as his favourite car. He won that title as Clark would have won it: all ease and precision and sublime confidence, his place in the sport now beyond reasonable argument.

Jackie Stewart's Matra rounds the Station hairpin at Monaco 1969. Although he retired from this race, six victories at other Grands Prix secured his first World Championship.

Jacky Ickx was the prodigy of the time, the one for whom all things seemed possible. This was the man who qualified third at the Nürburgring in 1967 – in a Formula 2 Matra – the man whose fearless antics in that race had Stewart begging Ken Tyrrell to slow him down before he hurt himself. His apprenticeship was fiery.

And yet he matured into one of racing's true artists, with an effortless and fluent style. It was no surprise that the unsubtle technique required by ground-effect cars did not suit him. History will remember Jacky primarily as a sports car driver, which is sad and does him no justice. There were days in Formula 1 when he simply left everyone standing, and probably there has never been anyone better in the wet.

He was always an individualist. Testing bored him, and so, essentially, did competition. He would tell you in that gravelly voice, that he always drove as if alone on the track, and he hoped it was faster than the others. The pleasure lay there, in seeing what was possible, in the battle between Ickx and himself.

WILLY MAIRESSE:
always over the top.

MIKE PARKES:
briefly impressive.

RICARDO RODRIGUEZ:
the genius of youth.

CHRIS AMON:
all talent, no luck.

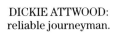

DICKIE ATTWOOD:
reliable journeyman.

MIKE SPENCE:
on the verge of the big time.

PIERS COURAGE:
by name and nature.

JOHNNY SERVOZ-GAVIN:
Gallic flair was not enough.

JACKIE OLIVER:
never front rank.

TREVOR TAYLOR:
Yorkshire grit personified.

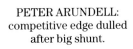

PETER ARUNDELL:
competitive edge dulled
after big shunt.

TONY MAGGS:
always a number two.

The undisputed master in the Fifties, Juan
Manuel Fangio drives the Mercedes-Benz
W196 in the 1954 Spanish Grand Prix. His total
of five World Championships is unlikely to be
surpassed.

The 1958 season was a tragic one for Scuderia
Ferrari, Peter Collins and Luigi Musso losing
their lives in accidents. Mike Hawthorn, seen
here at the Belgian Grand Prix, wrestled the
Championship from the grasp of Moss and
Vanwall by his consistent performances.
Within months, Britain's first World Champion
was also dead, the victim of a road accident.

Jack Brabham and Cooper led the rear-engined revolution; World Championships in 1959 and 1960 were their reward. His win at the 1960 Belgian Grand Prix (*right*) was just one of five successive victories that season.

American Phil Hill took the 1961 Drivers' title after his closest rival and team-mate Wolfgang von Trips was killed at Monza. This cast a shadow over what had hitherto been a triumphant season for Maranello. Hill is pictured here taking the 'shark-nose' Ferrari 156 V6 to third place in the Monaco Grand Prix.

Only Stirling Moss could challenge the might
of Ferrari in 1961, his victories at both Monaco
and the Nürburgring (*left*) with Rob Walker's
Lotus rank among Grand Prix racing's
greatest drives.

In 1962 BRM at last fulfilled their potential
and Graham Hill deservedly won the
Championship. His first ever Grand Prix win
came at the Dutch Grand Prix at Zandvoort.

Jim Clark and Lotus were synonymous: two World Championships were scant reward for his efforts, for 33 pole positions, 25 wins, 27 fastest laps and 274 points were achieved from just 72 starts.
Below: Clark on his way to victory in the 1963 French Grand Prix at Reims.

John Surtees – the only champion on both two wheels and four – snatched the title for Ferrari in 1964. The superb photo shows him at work in the Monaco Grand Prix the following season.

A unique achievement: at the age of 40 Jack Brabham won both the 1966 World Championships for Drivers and Constructors with his own car. He is shown below cruising to victory in the Dutch Grand Prix. Denis Hulme took the title for the Brabham team again in 1967.

Jackie Stewart amassed a record of 27 Grand Prix wins and three World Championships in a glittering career. He is pictured *right* in the Matra-Ford winning the 1969 Italian Grand Prix, while *below* he hurls his Tyrrell-Ford towards victory in the 1971 British Grand Prix on the way to his second Championship.

Jochen Rindt became the sport's first
posthumous World Champion after he was
killed in practice for the 1970 Italian Grand
Prix. He is seen struggling with the then
unsorted Lotus 72 at the Spanish Grand Prix
earlier in that season (*top*).

Above: Two years on the reliveried Lotus 72D
was still good enough to take a brilliant young
Emerson Fittipaldi to his first Championship.

Left: 1975 Champion Niki Lauda triumphed
again in 1977, his skill and courage against the
odds marked him as a true great. Here, 'Super
Rat' heads for victory in the Dutch Grand Prix
at Zandvoort.

Lauda's accident in the 1976 German Grand
Prix at the Nürburgring opened the door for
James Hunt, who took his opportunity
brilliantly to win the Championship by a
single point. Six victories were recorded with
the McLaren M23 including the Dutch Grand
Prix (*above*).

A familiar sight in 1978 – Lotus team-mates
Mario Andretti and Ronnie Peterson head the
field. For Mario the Championship was the
reward for his efforts in leading the Hethel
team out of the doldrums. The brilliant and
much loved Peterson was to die following an
accident at the start of the Italian Grand Prix,
the very race at which Mario clinched the title.

Champion in 1980, Alan Jones found the perfect team with Frank Williams and Patrick Head. Their partnership, which elevated the team from complete newcomers to champions, proved there was still room at the top for those with talent and dedication.

Jody Scheckter's ability marked him as a potential champion as early as 1973. This goal was finally achieved following a move to Ferrari in 1979. *Below,* he is shadowed by team-mate Gilles Villeneuve on his way to victory in the Monaco Grand Prix of that year.

lat
PEMEX
PEMEX
PEMEX
PEMEX
PEMEX
PEMEX
parmalat
PEMEX
parmalat
santal
5
parmalat
BRABHAM
GOODYEAR

Nelson Piquet (*left*) enjoyed a tremendous rapport with Brabham designer Gordon Murray and their partnership yielded two World titles in 1981 and 1983.

Keke Rosberg struggled to qualify the Fittipaldi in 1981, but a move to Williams saw him crowned World Champion the following season.

Niki Lauda pipped Alain Prost to the 1984 title by just half a point. The Marlboro-McLaren pair won 12 of the 16 races between them; Lauda's win at the Österreichring (*above*) was the only occasion on which he was to win his home Grand Prix.

After seven Grand Prix wins in 1984 and still no Championship, Alain Prost made no mistake the following year. His win at Monaco (*overleaf*) was just another step on the way to Championships in 1985 and 1986. The amiable Frenchman equalled Jackie Stewart's total of 27 victories at the 1987 Belgian Grand Prix, with the prospect of many more to follow.

THE SEVENTIES

By ALAN HENRY

**Ronnie Peterson locks a wheel on the March
approaching Druids Bend, Brands Hatch
1972.**

The veteran of France's rise to motor racing prominence in the 1960s, Jean-Pierre was a worker rather than an artist, many of his drives for Matra the product of a raw nationalistic fervour. Throughout 1968 and '69 he was content to remain in Jackie Stewart's shadow within the Matra squad, but took over as number one for the French team in 1970, using their own V12 engines. His greatest moment for the French team came at Clermont Ferrand that summer when it looked as though he had the French Grand Prix in the bag until the engine blew most of its oil away. In 1972 he drove for BRM and finally bagged his only Grand Prix win in torrential rain at Monaco, beating Jacky Ickx – acknowledged as the greatest wet-weather driver of his era – in a straight fight. It was proof that every driver has at least one great race within him. He never scaled such heights again, but kept racing saloon cars competitively for more than a decade after his F1 career came to an end. More than anything, JPB was a straightforward enthusiast.

Extrovert, charming and blessed with dazzling good looks, François Cevert was put on earth to be a racing driver. After enjoying considerable success in both F2 and F3, he was recruited to Formula 1 by Ken Tyrrell to partner Jackie Stewart early in 1970.

The bright-eyed young Frenchman proved a willing disciple of Stewart. By the summer of 1971 he was good enough to take second place behind JYS in the French Grand Prix and, with only a little luck, picked up a momentous victory at Watkins Glen later that year. Reckoned by some to be good enough to land a top drive elsewhere, Cevert remained an integral part of the Tyrrell family through 1972 and into '73. It was Ken's plan that Cevert would inherit Stewart's position as number one driver when JYS retired.

Sadly, that transition never happened. Battling with Ronnie Peterson for a front row starting position at the Glen, François Cevert was killed in a violent accident, and France had to wait for more than a decade before acclaiming its first World Champion.

Slotting almost perfectly into this section, Emerson's Grand Prix career began in 1970 highlighted by spectacular success. He won his fourth Grand Prix, the US race at Watkins Glen, to give Team Lotus a timely tonic following the tragic death of Jochen Rindt in practice at Monza. A decade later, it petered out almost unnoticed, driving for his own financially strapped team, his halcyon days all but forgotten.

Between those two divergent poles, Emerson Fittipaldi scaled terrific heights of success and plumbed depths of disappointment. An intuitive natural driver with great inborn skill and an analytical mind, he forged such a close bond with Colin Chapman that many were tempted to draw analogies with Jim Clark. It was Emerson who fully exploited the brilliant Lotus 72 to become the sport's youngest-ever World Champion – at the age of 23 in 1972 – but the lure of a lucrative Marlboro McLaren contract took him away from Lotus at the end of the following year, his morale slightly dented by the speed of his newly recruited team-mate Ronnie Peterson.

At McLaren he honed his driving style to perfection, handling the M23 with such consummate precision that it truly looked as though it was running on rails. He became Champion again in 1974 and was runner-up to the Ferrari-mounted Niki Lauda the following year. But Emerson had always harboured ambitions of forming his own team and, in partnership with his older brother Wilson, shook the Grand Prix world by quitting McLaren for their newly established Copersucar outfit at the start of 1976. It was a mistake.

A succession of designers and years of dogged trying failed to mould the Fittipaldi brothers' enterprise into anything approaching a front-running outfit. But there was one more day of F1 glory to come Emerson's way. In 1978, in front of his home crowd at Rio de Janeiro, he brought the Copersucar home a storming second to Reutemann's Ferrari. Sadly, the flame of Fittipaldi's unquestionable talent was never rekindled again at the wheel of a Grand Prix car. Looking back, Emerson's great gift was squandered on an emotional spur-of-the-moment decision in the autumn of 1975. He never quite achieved the status that his early exploits suggested he would, but the potential for greatness was there. He can still be seen racing competitively to this day on the US Indy car circuit.

Emerson Fittipaldi switched from Lotus to McLaren
for 1974 and claimed his second World
Championship.

To some he was regarded as the classic all-American hero. Others simply looked on him as a rich kid got lucky. By the time Peter Revson hit his first winning streak in Formula 1 he was over 30, having first sampled F1 with a private Lotus-BRM in the early 1960s.

'Revvie' was determined, aggressive on his day and quite a stylist. He signed up with McLaren at the start of 1972 but it was not until he was in the cockpit of the splendid M23 for the '73 season that he had a car to unlock the door to Formula 1 success. He judged things superbly at Silverstone in the British GP, running the gauntlet of a rain shower to beat Peterson, Hulme and Hunt past the flag by a few seconds. Later that season he added the confused Canadian GP to his victory tally. But he fell out with the team's management and quit to join the fledgling Shadow outfit for 1974.

A banal accident while testing at Kyalami snatched away the handsome American just as he was establishing himself as a serious front-runner. I always thought he had a lot more to give.

Relaxed, easygoing and good natured, Peter Gethin seemed to lack that ruthless edge which marks out a World Champion from the average F1 driver. Having served an apprenticeship in the fledgling Formula 5000, Peter was taken under the McLaren team's wing and got his full-time break when Bruce McLaren was killed in the summer of 1970. He seemed little more than a good, solid midfield performer and produced no results of consequence before moving to BRM in the middle of 1971. He wrote his name into the pages of motor racing history when he risked everything on an audacious dive down the inside of his rivals going into Parabolica on the last corner of the Italian Grand Prix at Monza, out-dragging Ronnie Peterson to the line to win by one-hundredth of a second. Heroic wasn't the word for it, but 'Geth' was destined never to win in F1 again. A chirpy, popular character, he survived to retire from the cockpit and still remains on the fringes of the sport to this day.

The Seventies

Jackie started the decade in a whirlwind of attention after winning his first championship at Monza with the Tyrrell Matra at the end of 1969. What followed next almost destroyed his self-confidence. Tyrrell had to become a March customer while the team's own car was secretly being completed and it turned out to be a ponderous truck by comparison with the agile Matra. Jackie almost worried himself to a standstill until the new Tyrrell appeared, allowing him to reassert his championship form in the last few races of the 1970 season.

But although Stewart cantered to the 1971 title, he lived a hectic business life in the fast lane and, alongside his motor racing, he was just taking too much out of himself. In 1972 he developed mononucleosis and a duodenal ulcer. Six weeks of enforced inactivity followed, during which his championship title slipped away yet again. In 1973 he won his third title and quit the cockpit at the end of the year, having made the decision to do so early in the season and keeping it a secret for several months.

As a driver, Jackie honed the fine edge of his talent during the second phase of his career, but at the same time emerged as a more pragmatic performer. He minimised the risks in ruthlessly dispassionate fashion, never over-driving emotionally when the odds were stacked overwhelmingly against him. But when everything clicked, Jackie Stewart could still display a rare brilliance right through to the closing months of his career. He will always be remembered as the great star who drained all emotion from his driving, something which failed to find favour with the traditionalists. Perhaps that's one of the reasons he is still around for us to enjoy his endearing brand of cockiness to this day.

Stewart's Tyrrell heads a young Niki Lauda in the
March during the rain-lashed 1972 Monaco Grand
Prix.

The Seventies

I first watched Niki Lauda in the European Formula 2 Trophy series in 1971 where this buck-toothed young Austrian's promise, skill and intelligence belied his inexperience. He moved into F1 on a 'rent-a-drive' basis the following year with March and it proved a humiliating experience which almost finished him once and for all. Once Niki had swollen the March bank balance he was left to sink or swim . . .

Ultimately, though, it was his pragmatic approach to the business side of motor racing which finally put him on the road to success. The way in which he coaxed and cajoled himself into the BRM team in 1973 gave us a foretaste of the razor-sharp commercial mind which would eventually help him become a millionaire from his chosen sport. Finally, he got the big break in '74 when he joined Ferrari, from which point he never looked back.

Shrewd, rational, methodical and able to make unemotional decisions, Niki Lauda quickly developed into the thinking man's Grand Prix driver of the 1970s. His rise to prominence was inextricably entwined with the Ferrari renaissance in the middle of the decade and, after a season's apprenticeship in 1974, he cantered to the championship the following year at the wheel of the splendid 312 *trasversale*. Then, in the summer of 1976, came his crash at the Nürburgring. He was badly burned about the head, but the damage to his lungs caused by scorching fumes did the most serious short-term damage. For a couple of days he hung precariously between life and death, but proceeded to make such a storming recovery that he was racing again in less than two months.

He failed to save his championship title from James Hunt's onslaught, but bounced back in 1977 to defeat not only his rivals to regain his title but also snubbed his nose at the 'Maranello mafia' who reckoned he was finished. At the end of the year he raised two fingers to Ferrari, leaving to join Brabham before retiring abruptly midway through practice for the 1979 Canadian Grand Prix. It seemed as though we had lost this remarkable personality for good to the world of aviation, but he was back in the cockpit just over two years later. As well as displaying total honesty, accurate self-appraisal and remarkable self-discipline, Niki Lauda was, on his day, also as *quick* as anybody on the track.

Niki Lauda rounds the Karussel on his way to third
place in the 1975 German Grand Prix at the
Nürburgring.

What many people failed to understand about Clay Regazzoni was his *passion* for racing. 'You must believe that, for me, winning is not as important as *being there*, being part of the scene', he used to say. After gaining early celebrity status as a Ferrari team member, he switched to BRM for an unsuccessful season in 1973 before being welcomed back into the Maranello fold again for 1974. He was woefully inconsistent, taken over his career as a whole, but when he clicked he had the potential to win. But when he was having a bad day, half the grid knew about it . . .

Kicked out of Ferrari at the end of 1976, his career path took him via Ensign and Shadow to Williams. In 1979 he won Frank's first-ever F1 success – at Silverstone – but was dropped in favour of Reutemann at the end of the year. Partly paralysed after an accident for which he was blameless at Long Beach in 1980, Clay was henceforth relegated to the sidelines. A passionate, emotive and erratic racer, the sport could do with more people like the roughish, moustachioed Swiss.

He was a perfectionist above all else. Enigmatic, serious and committed, Carlos Reutemann's personality was a baffling tangle of contradictions for much of his career. One day his brilliance would shine like a beacon and you were convinced he was the best driver of his era. The next weekend he would put in a pathetic performance, in no way worthy of his acknowledged status. He never managed to string together a successful title onslaught, but he was definitely serious championship material.

His successful formative years in F1 were spent with the Brabham team, but when Bernie Ecclestone switched to Alfa power, Carlos moved on to Ferrari where 1977 team-mate Lauda and Andretti in 1978 both threw the title beyond his reach.

In 1979 he switched to Lotus, but, again, it was the wrong decision. He raced on into the 1980s before giving it all up. Today he admits he retired too soon. A civilised and charming man, Carlos Reutemann basically failed to do justice to his own superb talent. But who can explain precisely why?

For much of his career, James seemed to treat his motor racing as a bit of a 'wizard wheeze' with plenty of birds and off-track boozing to make the party swing. But that was only a superficial view of the man's incredibly inconsistent form. There were days when he drove *brilliantly* – there's no other word for it – but one always had the feeling, rightly it turned out, that Formula 1 wasn't the be-all and end-all for the Wellington-educated racer.

James won his Grand Prix spurs with the Hesketh team where Bubbles Horsley should be given credit for bringing the best out of James, helping him immeasurably to mature as a driver. His victory in the '75 Dutch Grand Prix, where he beat Lauda's Ferrari in a straight fight, underlined the fact that there was more to Hunt than had met the eye during his chaotic early years in F3. The McLaren team was the beneficiary of his new-found maturity, as they drafted James into their ranks after Fittipaldi's defection to his family team. As history records, Hunt won the '76 title, but that stark fact conceals some terrific races. Nürburgring, Zandvoort, Mosport Park and Watkins Glen all fell to James in sparkling style. In 1977 he won several more Grand Prix victories, but McLaren was slow to climb aboard the ground-effect bandwagon and, faced with the prospect of assuming the role of also-ran, James's performances became rather patchy and unpredictable.

By the end of 1978 he was finished with McLaren and moved to join Walter Wolf's équipe. But he retired after a handful of races, unhappy about the way in which the latest breed of ground-effect cars were evolving with their rock hard suspension systems. A driver whose fans loved him dearly and detractors disliked him vehemently, James was always very much his own man. Even if you judged him lucky to win his sole World Championship title, he drove some fine individual races and remained resolutely and defiantly independent to the day he quit the sport.

Made in Japan . . . James Hunt's measured drive in
atrocious conditions at the Mount Fuji circuit
brought him the 1976 Championship.

An ideal and devoted team-mate to Mario Andretti, Gunnar's tragically brief career spanned only a couple of F1 seasons, but he left a sufficiently strong impression at Team Lotus to be remembered as an unusually talented rising star. He admired Mario enormously, had bags of raw enthusiasm and was happy learning his F1 trade at a time when Lotus was dragging itself out of a disappointing two-year run of poor equipment and missed opportunities.

In 1977, armed with the Lotus 78 'wing car', Gunnar drove a well-judged race in atrocious conditions to win the soaking Belgian Grand Prix at Zolder. He was a cheery soul with a gregarious nature, but his driving became patchy towards the end of the '77 season and it began to look as though he was finding the whole business physically taxing. What we did not know at the time was that he had the early symptoms of cancer. He signed to drive for the Arrows team in 1978, but was never well enough to race the car. He battled manfully against his illness throughout the summer and finally died in the autumn. It was a bitter loss.

Bernie Ecclestone isn't exactly renowned for his love of racing drivers. Catch him in the right mood and he will confess that in the last thirty years there have been perhaps four he has really had a lot of time for. One of them was Carlos Pace. In fact, Bernie once said 'if Carlos had lived, then I wouldn't have needed Niki Lauda'. That stands as the most eloquent testimony to the debonair Brazilian whose sole Grand Prix victory came in front of his home crowd at Interlagos in 1975. Armed with Bernie's compact Brabham BT44B, 'Moco' Pace beat fellow Paulistano Emerson Fittipaldi's McLaren in a straight fight. The scenes of delight that followed made Ferrari victory celebrations at Monza seem like a tea party on the vicarage lawn.

An obviously gifted rising star, Pace served his F1 apprenticeship with Williams and Surtees before joining Brabham midway through 1974. When the team switched to Alfa power he persevered doggedly with the project, in contrast to team-mate Reutemann who just gave up all hope. The whole project was just coming right when Pace died in a private plane crash near São Paulo shortly after the 1977 South African Grand Prix.

An incurable romantic, I always thought Jochen arrived in F1 about 20 years after the era which would have best suited him. Sensitive, intelligent and caring, this pleasant German was a fine racing driver, but allowed himself to be psychologically undermined by unsympathetic team managers and team-mates. He was never quite a number one, but emerged as one of the best number twos in the game, particularly at McLaren before he was worn down by a combination of James Hunt and Teddy Mayer, with neither of whom he could really hit it off. After his halcyon days at McLaren – during which he won the tragic, shortened 1975 Spanish race at Barcelona – he joined ATS and Arrows. The saddest moment came when he was involved in Gilles Villeneuve's fatal practice accident at Zolder in 1982. Disillusioned and saddened, he quit F1 at the end of the year. He is still regarded with enormous affection by those who were lucky enough to know him.

This dogged Italian driver was a rough old number, pushed on throughout his career by an obsessive and unquenchable enthusiasm for driving way over his head. But he got so much pure pleasure from his sport – seemingly even when crashing – that he became one of the most popular personalities in the pit lane. To be frank, Vittorio made Andrea de Cesaris look cool and composed. But he was quick on his day, planting his March on pole position for the 1975 Swedish Grand Prix, and when he won the rain-reduced, half-distance Austrian Grand Prix he crossed the line punching the air so enthusiastically that he promptly lost control and spun into the guard rail just beyond the finishing line. In some ways he was a one-man disaster area, but the crowd loved him and F1 insiders were always kept entertained by the innocent way in which he tried to explain away his errors. Despite being hurt in the multiple shunt which cost Ronnie Peterson his life at Monza in 1978, Vittorio happily recovered to retire from the sport in one piece. A thoroughly good bloke.

A man with star quality stamped through his personality like a stick of Brighton rock. Charismatic, civilised and every inch a racing driver, Mario Andretti's victory in the 1978 World Championship was but one facet of a career which embodied every imaginable category of the sport.

He kicked off his F1 successes with victory for Ferrari in the 1971 South African Grand Prix, but it was not until 1976 that he really gave F1 his undivided attention, helping Colin Chapman haul the team back from the edge of technical oblivion. Then came Lotus's pioneering work at the start of the ground-effect era and two magnificent seasons, 1977 and '78. To see him at work in the magnificent Lotus 79 was a rare glimpse of man and machine in total harmony. Car and driver almost talked to each other, forging a technical bond which paid off superbly. Chapman likened their special relationship to that which he had enjoyed with Jim Clark.

Mario was a natural talent, his gift spiced by a streak of impetuosity which perhaps reflected his Italian origins. Occasionally he would become over-excited in the first-lap scramble and make a fundamental error which would cost him the race. But the credits overwhelmingly outweighed the debits. It was a shame to watch him struggling with sub-standard equipment as Lotus's technical advantage evaporated into 1979 and '80.

Eventually, he spent his final F1 season with Alfa Romeo, but it amounted to a complete waste of time. By then over 40, he returned to concentrate his efforts on Indy car racing, but could never quite leave F1 alone. In 1982 he was offered a 'guest' appearance in a Ferrari 126 turbo at Monza. It was a truly emotional moment, like some sort of symbolic homecoming of a long-exiled hero. He planted it on pole position to round off a Grand Prix career which still glitters brightly in the mind's eye almost a decade after his title success. Sheer class sums it all up . . .

Mario Andretti enjoyed mixed fortunes during his
two seasons at Ferrari. He is pictured *above* leading
Pedro Rodriguez in the 1971 Spanish Grand Prix.

The good-looking Swede seemed set for stardom from the moment he first climbed into an F1 cockpit. Three barren seasons with the March team left him hungry for success, so when he joined Team Lotus to handle the brilliant type 72 as Emerson Fittipaldi's team-mate in 1973, the world held its breath...

Nobody was disappointed. His thrilling car control had Chapman's baby dancing on the outer limits of adhesion round every track on which it raced. But the World Championship eluded him. He stayed with Lotus for the next two years, but as the team lost its technical edge, his extrovert driving style became progressively more frantic as prospects of further victories evaporated. His moves to March (1976) and Tyrrell (1977) were unproductive, but an opportunity to rebuild his reputation came in 1978 when he rejoined Lotus – as number two to Mario Andretti. It was a dignified decision made by an honourable man. When he died from injuries sustained in a startline pile-up at Monza the F1 world was pole-axed. Nobody ever had a bad word to say against Ronnie, for as well as being a terrific racer he was quite simply a lovely guy.

Patrick Depailler was the 'little boy lost' amongst the generation of French new-boys led by François Cevert in the early 1970s. Genial, slightly nervous, but totally embroiled in the business of motor racing, this slightly-built Frenchman seemed destined to be cast in the role of supporting star for much of his career. But a win a Monaco in 1978 boosted his reputation and, when Guy Ligier expanded his operation to run a second car in 1979, Patrick was picked to partner Jacques Laffite. He won the Spanish Grand Prix, but then injured himself badly by crashing a hang glider and was invalided out for the rest of the year. Bloody minded tenacity dragged him back to the cockpit for 1980, only for Patrick to be killed testing his Alfa Romeo at Hockenheim. It was a tragic waste.

Early in his career they called him 'Baby Bear' because he was schooled by Denny 'The Bear' Hulme during his first few races with McLaren. Later he was nicknamed 'Fletcher' after the over-ambitious baby seagull in the book *Jonathan Livingstone Seagull* who was always trying to fly before he was ready to, inevitably crashing into the pit face as a result. He exploded onto the European scene in 1971, driving Formula Ford, and by the end of the following season was making his F1 debut at the wheel of a McLaren at Watkins Glen. By the summer of '73 he could be seen leading the French Grand Prix at Paul Ricard – and destroying half the pack a few weeks later as he triggered a multi-car pile-up which brought the British Grand Prix to a premature halt!

Most people thought Jody would never live to a ripe old age. Despite his obvious lack of experience, the cocky South African set such a fearsome pace in those early days that most watched his progress with their hands partially covering their eyes, waiting for The Big Shunt. Thankfully, it never happened and Jody settled down in 1974 to drive three seasons with Ken Tyrrell. He won a handful of Grands Prix, but by the end of '76, many people believed he had lost his edge. He proved them wrong in 1977, winning three races for the revitalised Walter Wolf team and coming within sniffing distance of the championship.

In 1979 he moved to Ferrari. Most touchline observers thought this was the end. That stroppy South African and all those hysterical Italians – a recipe for disaster. Not so! 'Fletch' got on famously at Maranello and won the World Championship, despite having Gilles Villeneuve as his team-mate. At the end of the following year he retired, barely 30 years old. He matured into a relaxed, popular campaigner with an appealing, slightly world-weary sense of humour. And in the cockpit, he had it all nicely worked out, wiping away his early impulsiveness and replacing it with a controlled aggression that worked well for him.

Jody Scheckter won in Sweden and collected points consistently in 1976 with the amazing six-wheeled Tyrrell. He heads for third place in the Belgian Grand Prix *(above)*.

Introspective and modest, Jean-Pierre Jabouille's fleeting taste of Grand Prix success came hand-in-hand with the rise of Renault as a Formula 1 force. A methodical test driver blessed with a disarmingly easy temperament, he helped bring the French team's turbo efforts to fruition over two years of painstaking development. The reward for all this effort was victory in the French Grand Prix at Dijon in 1979, followed up by a disciplined and well-judged win, by a second or so, from Alan Jones's Williams at the Öster-reichring the following summer. That latter race demonstrated Jabouille's true calibre. Armed with a much faster car, he did the minimum necessary to keep Jones off the victory rostrum. No drama, no heroics, just the sensible use of the machinery beneath him.

Signed by Ligier for 1981, he sustained serious leg injuries in his Renault at Montreal in his last-but-one race for the team. It knocked the stuffing out of him. Although he returned to the cockpit, he was never the same driver and retired after a handful of races.

His sheer *joie-de-vivre* and zest for life has always been infectious. His driving reflected the competitiveness of his car. As Keke Rosberg, his team-mate for two years at Williams, explained, 'Give Jacques the best car and he'll run at the front. Give him the worst and he will be nowhere.' Jacques' driving style was smooth and crisp, with an artistic flow that made you think he could have developed into a great driver. But he was never serious enough for that. Life was for living and motor racing was part of that life. But only part of it. He had no hang-ups and, even when well over 40, occasionally looked a potential winner in his Ligier-Renault.

A great friend of Alain Prost, with whom he would use almost any excuse to nip off early after practice in order to play golf, Jacques retains a keen and unquenchable sense of humour which endured through a painful recovery from the accident which ended his career at Brands Hatch in 1986. At Dallas in 1984 the race morning warm-up took place at 7.30 a.m. Jacques arrived at the circuit wearing only his pyjamas. That said it all about the guy . . .

If you'd watched Tony Brise shaking his fist as he tried to lap his Embassy Hill team-mate Alan Jones in the rain-soaked 1975 Dutch Grand Prix, you might have come to the conclusion that the Australian wasn't much cop. But, as with so many self-made stars, Alan only needed some half-decent equipment under him to make his mark. Out in the wilderness with no apparent future, he got his big chance with Shadow after Tom Pryce was killed at the start of 1977, and picked up a lucky win in that summer's Austrian Grand Prix. Clearly, he was performing better than the Shadow and his bulldog tenacity earned him a place in the revitalised Williams team for 1978. When Patrick Head designed the world-beating ground-effect Williams FW07, Alan squeezed every last ounce of potential out of it. A true child of the ground-effect era, Jones displayed tremendous consistency, iron nerve and an unremitting will to win. He was a fighter more than an artist, but a ferociously determined one at that.

Ending on a high note. Alan Jones leads the pack into the first corner of the 1981 Las Vegas Grand Prix to record a final victory in his last race for Williams before retirement. His subsequent reappearances failed to meet with the same success.

This popular Ulsterman always seemed to make life more complicated for himself than it needed to be. His was a terrific natural talent which, like Reutemann's, never really came to full flower, though for different reasons. John was perpetually trying to rationalise and over-analyse his own personal race performances and was such a perfectionist that he tended to fiddle round with chassis settings chasing some elusive compromise, rather than going out and hurling the car about by the scruff of its neck.

Paradoxically, when John really got the wind up his tail he was a hard man to beat. His blend of skill and speed was probably at its peak in 1977 and '78 whilst driving the Brabham-Alfas, cars which habitually let him down. The French Grand Prix in '77 was a classic example, his BT45B hiccupping low on fuel two corners from home. He should have won that race – but then those six words encapsulate the story of John's F1 life.

JEAN-PIERRE JARIER:
Moody, inconsistent, but very
quick on his day.

MARK DONOHUE:
Experienced, methodical and
restrained. His death was due
to causes unfairly outside his
control.

TONY BRISE:
So much more to offer.

ROGER WILLIAMSON:
Rugged rising star killed
before his prime.

TOM PRYCE *(right):*
One of Britain's lost F1
generation.

HANS STUCK
(below): Magnificent
car control, but short
on singlemindedness.
The talent was there,
but not the
commitment.

MIKE HAILWOOD
(below): A sunny and
uninhibited character
whose innate
brilliance never got the
chance to shine
through on four
wheels.

ROLF STOMMELEN
(bottom): His early
promise was never
quite sustained.

**Fierce rivals: Nigel Mansell's Williams-Honda
leads Ayrton Senna's Lotus-Renault at the
1986 French Grand Prix.**

Talking to him, you would never have known this was the most naturally gifted driver of his day. Watch him on the track and there would be no doubt.

Gilles Villeneuve had spine-tingling flair. It was an asset which he exploited to the full, largely because he enjoyed the sensation of sliding a racing car under power. That raw enthusiasm reached the spectators, giving the feeling this was not merely work; it was *fun*. But that should not suggest that Villeneuve was foolhardy. In his own way, he was totally dedicated to winning.

There were no big egos when Gilles was around. Devoid of pretension, Villeneuve preferred to stay with his wife and children in a camper, which he would park in the paddock. The Ferrari mechanics, for whom he drove almost exclusively in Formula 1, adored him for it.

He died at Zolder in May 1982, giving his all in a Ferrari. Some said that he was reckless, that he had it coming. Others, with a deeper appreciation of his genius, felt no comment was necessary. Gilles Villeneuve's input to motor racing during an all too brief period had said it all.

Here was the man who had everything: boyish good looks, a strong physique, style both on and off the track, and a works Ferrari drive to boot. All told, it gave him confidence . . . a great deal of confidence.

In August 1982, he was leading the championship by nine points. Nothing, it seemed, could stop him. Fastest in practice on the first day of the German Grand Prix, he went out the following morning in pouring rain. Fastest again. Then he crashed, the severe leg injuries ending his career right there, on the fast approach to the Hockenheim stadium.

The thing about Didier Pironi was that, had he succeeded in 1982, he could have won the championship again and again. His supreme talent and clean-cut appearance guaranteed a place in the plans of any top-drawer team or sponsor. He was well-educated, soft-spoken and mild-mannered. Yet he barely acknowledged his mechanics while racing for Tyrrell, the team which brought him into Formula 1 in 1978. Underneath the acceptable facade was a ruthless determination to get his way.

For Pironi, 1982 was a messy, unhappy ending to a Grand Prix career blessed by artistic skill but backed by a rather chilling lack of emotion.

If this book had been published before March 1986, the page devoted to Nelson Piquet might have told a different story. It would have been a eulogy about a Brazilian acquainted with success and very little failure during seven years in Formula 1. There would have been 13 Grand Prix wins and two World Championships; a relationship with the Brabham team which amounted to kinship.

Brabham, devoted to their driver, looked upon Nelson as a complete natural. He probably still is but a lot has changed since joining Williams in 1986. He has been beaten fair and square by his team-mate. Apart from the early days alongside Niki Lauda, that has never happened to him before. It seemed to take Nelson's army of supporters by surprise – not to mention the man himself.

Unfortunately, it has tainted the reputation of a driver previously bracketed alongside the world's greats. Now you'll be hard-pressed to find him included in anyone's all-time Top Ten. Perhaps that's because Nelson's recent plight at the hands of Nigel Mansell has put the difficulty of assessing a driver's ability into sharp relief. Certainly, it has made the pundits, myself included, look foolish and the temptation is to ease Nelson Piquet into the background and pretend his heyday as Number One in the *Autocourse* Top Ten never existed.

But it did and Nelson's contribution to the sport is immense. His greatest asset, apart from an affinity with a car at speed, is that he simply loves driving. It is a quality which designers dream about. Nelson will happily spend hours pounding around a test track; there's nothing else that he wants to do. Except, perhaps, sleep.

Nelson is never satisfied unless he has packed in a solid ten hours of slumber and maybe that has contributed towards his indolent nature. Not a man for public relations and bonhomie, Piquet retreats to Monte Carlo and disappears in his boat which is, needless to say, without a phone.

Piquet hates the glitter and trappings of success. While other drivers would rush off to the Boss factory to kit themselves out in expensive clothes, Nelson, dressed in a Mickey Mouse sweatshirt and blue jeans, would be found at Hockenheim, hanging around the Brabham team, playing a leading role in nurturing the family atmosphere within it. Then he went to Williams and was paid his worth. Whether he earned it or not has been one of the great debates of recent years and that's a sad way to reflect on a brilliant past.

Nelson Piquet joined Williams-Honda for 1986 with
a third World Championship in prospect, only to
find himself upstaged by team-mate Nigel Mansell.
Above he leads Michele Alboreto at Monza on his
way to victory in the 1986 Italian Grand Prix.

The initial impressions were good. When the news came through that a young Italian had lapped the Nürburgring north circuit at a dazzling speed in a Formula 3 car, it was obvious that this was a man apart. For a start, he had never raced there before. And, even if he had, lapping the 'Ring quickly called for a mixture of commitment and skill which sorts the men from the boys.

We were not disappointed when Riccardo Patrese made his GP debut in a Shadow at Monaco in '77; not the easiest of cars, not the easiest of F1 circuits. He made few mistakes and finished ninth. Grand Prix wins and a championship or two seemed assured. So what went wrong?

Patrese, at the time of writing, has won two Grands Prix. Neither of them can be considered a classic in the sense that he thoroughly deserved the result. In a way, it sums up the rest of his career with Arrows, Alfa Romeo and Brabham. Somehow, the motivation has been suspect, certainly incapable of matching and moulding his natural talent. It is almost in keeping with a private, unobtrusive man whose passion away from the race track is model railways. He may be a potential winner but, in the Italian tradition, he is likely to leave the rails at the wrong moment.

When awarded the Renault drive which brought him into Grand Prix racing full time, René Arnoux cried. It was indicative of a man of emotion, most of which the Grand Prix world has never fully understood, try as they might.

René Arnoux is a strange mixture of an earthy talent and agricultural habits. His casual attire may reflect a nonchalant air as he trudges through the paddock but, once in the car, a fiery nature has accounted for brilliant drives and belligerent behaviour, sometimes in the same afternoon.

Despite his provincial accent, the chic French F1 set had no complaints when he won four Grands Prix and took 14 pole positions for Renault. That natural car control was what attracted the attention of Enzo Ferrari.

Moving to Maranello was, perhaps, René's biggest mistake. The Italian habit of deifying Ferrari drivers suited him too well. He left behind his wife and family and, it seemed, a good deal of sound judgement. There were three wins plus a brilliant second place earned purely on reflex at Dallas. But there were also inexplicable moments; inconsistent actions. In the end, the move to a more relaxed environment at Ligier better suited a carefree character with more to offer than a wild-eyed look.

There's a classic shot taken during the North American Formula Atlantic series in the late Seventies. It shows Keke Rosberg in full opposite lock, a front wheel pawing the air. The rear of his Chevron, apart from struggling for grip as the throttle remains planted to the floor, is kissing a concrete wall. The car, painted pink, is sponsored by Excita Condoms.

Rosberg was doing this sort of thing 41 times in the space of 36 weekends during the summer of 1978. Not possible? It is if you possess the incredible ebullience of a man who appeared to work by the creed 'the only time I was beaten was when I wasn't there'.

Keke Rosberg was a motor racing paradox. On the one hand, he was a professional who never paid for a drive throughout his career. On the other, he broke every rule in the racing school textbook. His progress around the circuit would be accompanied by a frantic blipping of the throttle, the car jumping over kerbs, its front wheels rarely pointing in the direction of travel, the action in the cockpit a blur.

Yet it was this controlled violence which made Keke such compelling viewing. The Jackie Stewarts of this world may have shaken their heads in despair but the crowd loved it. Anyone who witnessed Rosberg's 160 mph pole-position lap at Silverstone in 1985 will testify to that.

It's unfortunate that Keke's record will be tainted by just a single win in 1982, his championship year. All told, it was an untidy season, but the fact remains that Keke made the most of it. He was used to that.

No-one bothered much about the cocky little Finn with the extrovert style until Frank Williams took him on as a last-minute replacement for Carlos Reutemann. In many ways, it was a marriage of convenience but Keke grabbed his chance and, within seven months, he had won the title. How he did it was of no consequence since the principle objective was to apply a shrewd mind to the business of being World Champion.

Rosberg, acutely aware of the role of commerce in motor sport, loved the wheeling and dealing. Sponsors paid their whack but they were delighted with Keke's input while rubbing shoulders with guests in the hospitality areas and mixing it with his colleagues on the track. His stamina for all manner of work was astonishing. A heavy smoker, his healthy disregard for po-faced convention was as refreshing as a wry, almost wicked, sense of humour. But it was that urgent, totally committed style in a racing car which suited him best.

The 1985 Australian race was to be Keke Rosberg's final Grand Prix win for Williams. His move to McLaren proved to be a major disappointment.

When protesting drivers locked themselves in a Johannesburg hotel in 1982, Elio de Angelis soothed many a frayed nerve by playing classical music on a piano. In some ways, that musical talent seemed better suited to his gentle, polite manner than was the hurly-burly of Formula 1. Yet Elio had the handsome, Italian cut of a racing driver, and even if his hunger to succeed may not have been as sharp as that of some of his rivals, he used that same finger-tip flair to take his car to the limit.

Perhaps his best days were with Shadow in 1979. Agreed, money had got him that far but he had something to prove and used his inherent ability to work an uncompetitive car into places where it ought not to have been.

After that, Lotus and Brabham – and two Grand Prix wins. It is an inappropriate epitaph to a charming, highly skilled racing driver who felt that there was a little more to life than Formula 1. And that made his death during a test session at Paul Ricard in 1986 seem all the more unnecessary.

The highlight of his career is likely to be a win at Imola, driving Ferrari number 27, the car which previously belonged to Gilles Villeneuve. When Gilles died, Tambay was chosen as his friend's replacement. It was, in Patrick's eyes, an honour and he did it justice by avenging Villeneuve's defeat at Imola the previous year. To any other driver, it would simply have been a very nice win. For Patrick Tambay, it was almost preordained, such was his sensitive nature.

That acute awareness, of course, got him in the end. There is no room for nice guys in Formula 1 and Tambay was, unquestionably, a gentleman. French by birth, a period in the United States gave him a delightful accent and a fluency in English. A former ski champion, Patrick looked every inch a Grand Prix driver. He played it too, particularly when Ferrari salvaged a career which appeared to be snared by his self-effacing manner.

There were low periods with McLaren and Ligier. But, when on top form, believing fully in himself and a first-rate car, Tambay was unbeatable. Unfortunately for motor racing, those days were all too rare.

The Eighties

The story about the car wash has been told many times, but it bears repeating. Trophies, by and large, were meaningless to Niki Lauda and he reached an agreement with his local garage. They could display the silverware in their window in return for free car washes. Business is business and it was always so from the moment Niki Lauda arranged a £30,000 loan to buy his way into Formula 1.

Lauda's cold, commercial approach seemed to extend to his driving. There was no tingling excitement about it; no opposite lock. There was a job to be done and the motivation was doing it better than anyone else. Power slides and tyre smoke were all very well – but they were a waste of time and effort, a diversion from the realisation of the perfect lap in practice and nine points at the end of the weekend's work. Earn enough points and you win the championship. You can keep the trophies.

By the summer of 1979, the garage was decked out with the trappings of two World Championships and 17 wins. What next? The realisation that there was little else to achieve dawned about 11.0 on the morning of 28 September during practice for the Canadian Grand Prix. By 11.30, Niki Lauda, retired racing driver, was on his way to the airport to pursue the challenge of expanding his commercial airline, Lauda Air.

At 30, he had been, in his words, to hell and back. A terrible accident at the Nürburgring in 1976 had almost killed him. The second championship less than a year later was a startling display of mind over matter. It was almost as if the need to recover had itself provided the necessary stimulant. It was the same when he revitalised the shambling Ferrari team in 1974. It was the same when he returned to watch a Formula 1 race in 1981.

Now we had ground-effect cars which called for physical fitness and a totally different driving technique. This was new to Lauda and his curiosity was primed. Was it possible to come back and drive one of these cars? Could he win a race again? He was hooked. Like a man flirting with a jilted lover merely to keep her hopes alive and boost his ego, Lauda returned to prove he could assert his will over these infinitely more difficult cars.

It *was* different but that was the very reason why he relished the challenge; why further wins were almost a foregone conclusion. When he clinched the championship with McLaren for a third time at Estoril in 1984, that toothy grin said as much as the scarred face which told of a remarkable man who had seen and done it all. For the time being . . .

Comebacks are usually a bad idea, but Niki Lauda
returned to claim a third championship. His
McLaren wins the 1984 British Grand Prix at Brands
Hatch *(above)*.

'I knew,' said Jackie Stewart, 'that my record would go one day. The thing is that I didn't want it to go to a driver who had gone on and on and somehow reached 28 wins. I wanted it to go to someone who deserved it. And I can think of no-one better than Alain Prost. To my mind, he's the best there is out there today.'

Prost wasn't always held in such high regard. Somehow, his efforts with the Renault team will always be associated with a failure to win the championship in 1983. Yet, in retrospect, most of his nine Grands Prix wins for the French team must be considered remarkable.

At the time it seemed too easy. That has been the hallmark of Alain Prost's progress around any track you care to mention. The fluency which the Frenchman brings to a winning drive makes it look simple; the good grace with which he accepts defeat makes that look easy too. In fact, both disciplines call for immense self-control from a man who loves winning.

That has been his creed from the days spent hanging around the Grand Prix paddocks, his status as European Formula 3 Champion strengthening a resolve to break into Formula 1. I remember interviewing him at the time. 'What's your ambition?' I asked, rather blandly. 'To be World Champion, of course', he replied, looking at me as though I had asked Enzo Ferrari if he was interested in motor racing.

This burning desire has been tempered with enough common sense to turn down a drive with McLaren in a third car at Watkins Glen in 1979. Many would have grabbed the opportunity and thought about the repercussions of inexperience later. But not Prost. He did eventually join McLaren and the move to Renault after just one year was a leap out of the frying pan into the fire. The wins were almost in spite of the efforts of driving for a committee and Prost's true value was not established until a return to the revamped McLaren team in 1984.

Now he was with an organisation which shared his enthusiasm for achieving the last millimetre of perfection when it came to setting up a car. After that, his driving became a finely honed balance of aggression and tactics. The only thing left was to adjust his attitude outside business hours. Golf, introduced by his good friend Jacques Laffite, became the ideal relaxation. After that, the championship in 1985 never seemed in doubt. But, as his chewed finger nails will testify, winning and seeking the perfect lap remain the ultimate aim.

Certainly the driver of the Eighties and possibly the best ever? Alain Prost clocks up victories with apparent ease; this, his 27th, at the 1987 Belgian Grand Prix equalled Jackie Stewart's long-standing record.

In a preview for the 1987 British Grand Prix, a journalist wrote: 'Ayrton Senna: is this man crazy?' Anyone dreaming up a headline like that has clearly not made the acquaintance of a driver who lives, breathes and, when he reluctantly tears himself away from his team, sleeps motor racing.

There is nothing crazy about Ayrton Senna. Quite the opposite. His ambition is to win the World Championship, something which he has had in mind since joining Formula 1 with Toleman in 1984. And, from the outset, those associated with him could not doubt such a logical conclusion, given his precocious skill and a hunger to succeed which takes some believing.

The problem is, people interpret Senna's articulation of his beliefs as arrogance. He is merely stating the truth as he sees it. Ayrton keeps himself to himself at the race track; nothing must divert him from the job in hand. Mechanics are sometimes shocked by Senna's abrupt way of dealing with them if they make a mistake. Again, he is simply pointing out the error of their ways, not in a malicious sense, but as a means to an end — which is winning.

Brilliant? Yes. Naïve? Sometimes. Crazy? No.

Golfers marvel at Nigel Mansell's handicap of two. They also say he possesses very little style yet he commands that ball with a physical determination and a straight eye which are devastating in their effectiveness.

It is the same with his motor racing. For most critics, it just doesn't seem right, somehow, that Mansell should be so good. Yet there he is, paralysing former World Champions in identical cars. Perhaps it's his demeanour *out* of the car that's the problem: the sweating, the excuses, the aches and pains, the whispering with associates.

Mansell's homely, honest character is matched by a firm handshake and an unfailing politeness. At the end of the day, you can't take that away from him any more than you can discount his results on the track. He may have spent more than 70 Grands Prix bouncing from retirement to near-miss but, since that day at Brands Hatch in 1985, he has become a *winner*. And he's done it with a sense of dedication and self-belief which makes the mere word persistence seem an insult. Mansell's success has been thoroughly well-deserved and worked for the hard way.

The nice thing about Gerhard Berger is that he didn't arrive in Formula 1 with stars in his eyes and big numbers in his head. He knew, simply, that he was quick and, when you feel that way, it's not necessary to indulge in the bowing and scraping performed by less skilful members of his profession.

Berger's enthusiasm tumbles out of the car. That was particularly evident when he picked up the Arrows by the scruff of the neck in 1985 and caught the eye of the top teams. A year with Benetton in 1986 gave him a Grand Prix win and appeared to vindicate the call from Ferrari.

Berger accepted. It was in keeping with his dashing image although somehow at odds with his other occupation as the owner of a successful haulage company in his native Austria. Perhaps, in a flush of youth and inexperience, he rushed in too soon. But, then, you would hardly have expected otherwise from Gerhard Berger.

How can you possibly come from Milan, drive for Ferrari, win Grands Prix – and be as equable and placid as Michele Alboreto? More to the point, how can you *lose* for Ferrari and yet keep your head while those around you in the national press appear to be losing theirs?

Michele Alboreto understands the Italians better than they understand themselves. His empathy is converted into a mechanical sympathy while in the car. Mechanics marvel at the state of his gearbox at the end of a hard race. You can hear the smooth gearchanges for yourself, see the flowing lines through the corners, witness a graceful fluency which was hammered into competitive shape by Ken Tyrrell.

Michele won races for Ken in Las Vegas and Detroit, and the Tyrrell mechanics still speak fondly of the shy, mop-topped young man who took the trouble to visit the team's headquarters and present each member of the workforce with a parting gift at the end of 1983. Now he is public property and his value on the streets of Italy is set by wins, nothing less.

THIERRY BOUTSEN: Quiet
but very determined; a future
World Champion.

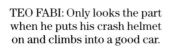

TEO FABI: Only looks the part
when he puts his crash helmet
on and climbs into a good car.

DEREK WARWICK:
Street-wise and a hard racer.

MARTIN BRUNDLE: Former
car salesman and a
no-nonsense professional.

STEFAN JOHANSSON:
Bubbling ability to drive fast
and tell jokes.

EDDIE CHEEVER:
Looks and sounds very fast.

ANDREA DE CESARIS: Quick, but more than his fair share of chances and crashes.

BRUNO GIACOMELLI: Italian comedian who never got to grips with Formula 1.

STEFAN BELLOF: A great talent lost before it could be fully appreciated.

MARC SURER: An excellent number two and a nice guy.

CRITICS TOP TEN

DENIS JENKINSON

NIGEL ROEBUCK

ALAN HENRY

MAURICE HAMILTON

1. **Jim Clark**

2. **Alberto Ascari**

3. **Stirling Moss**

4. **Juan Manuel Fangio**

5. **Mario Andretti**

6. **Gilles Villeneuve**

7. **Jackie Stewart**

8. **Ayrton Senna**

9. **Nelson Piquet**

10. **Alain Prost**

Choosing a Top Ten of drivers over a period of 37 years is not really practical, for few writers have been able to cover Grand Prix racing since the inception of the FIA World Championship. The life of a Grand Prix driver has changed considerably, too. In the 1950s a works driver took part in F1, F2, sports car racing, saloon car and GT racing, even hill-climbs and Indianapolis, so he had to be a true all-rounder. At times there were only seven or eight World Championship events, which allowed plenty of time to drive in other types of event. Today, with sixteen championship events and innumerable test days, a front rank works driver has no opportunity to do anything else, even if his contract allowed it.

If statistics were the only criteria then Alain Prost, with his record number of wins, and Juan Fangio with his record number of championships would top the list, whereas Stirling Moss would not rank very high, nor such outstanding 'natural' drivers as Villeneuve and Senna.

In choosing my Top Ten I have taken into account a driver's all-round ability, but of greater importance is the *way* he won races, regardless of championship points. Villeneuve had the right attitude and that was to win *all* the races, then being World Champion would automatically follow. Jimmy Clark, Stirling Moss and Alberto Ascari had the same outlook. If they were in a race, they were in it to win.

To my mind *winning* is the name of the game, not finishing first, and a true champion should dominate all the opposition at all times.

1. **Stirling Moss**

2. **Jim Clark**

3. **Alain Prost**

4. **Alberto Ascari**

5. **Juan Manuel Fangio**

6. **Jackie Stewart**

7. **Gilles Villeneuve**

8. **Ronnie Peterson**

9. **Niki Lauda**

10. **Jochen Rindt**

Moss I place first because, as a driver, he seemed to have no weaknesses whatever. An immaculate stylist, he was none the less a consummate racer. Whatever the conditions, whatever the circumstances, he was always *there*. And when did he ever have an 'off' day?

Clark gets the nod, just, over Prost because he so completely dominated his era – although you could argue that his era was easier to dominate than the Frenchman's. Jim usually had the best car, and was sometimes fallible under pressure. Prost I consider on a different plane from any of his contemporaries today.

Perhaps most would rate Fangio above Ascari, but, again, the Argentine invariably had the best car, and when he didn't (as in 1956 with Ferrari) his sheer driving superiority was less in evidence. Ascari, when he had the best equipment, as in 1952/53, cleaned up, but was perhaps even greater when up against it. And I'm sure he was the fastest of his time.

Into the top half-dozen has to come Stewart, like Prost a racer when he needed to be, but one who more often simply took control of a race; a driver of huge intelligence and savvy.

Villeneuve won only half a dozen races in his short career, and *never* had a car comparable with the best. Sometimes irrational on the track, his God-given talent ranks with any, and he never gave in. He was, I believe the *fastest* there has ever been.

Peterson and Rindt, who sandwich Lauda, had Villeneuve's *brio*, albeit in lesser measure. Like him, they had the ability, the genius, to win in cars not truly up to it. Like him, they stirred spectators as few ever did. Lauda is here because of the sheer weight of his achievement; never the fastest, yet always the brightest.

1. **Alain Prost**

2. **Jim Clark**

3. **Juan Manuel Fangio**

4. **Jackie Stewart**

5. **Stirling Moss**

6. **Alberto Ascari**

7. **Gilles Villeneuve**

8. **Niki Lauda**

9. **Ronnie Peterson**

10. **Graham Hill**

Naturally, I thought long and hard before placing today's top driver, Alain Prost, at number one ahead of such a legendary figure as Jim Clark. But at the end of the day I reasoned that Prost probably won a greater percentage of his races against superior opposition, both from the technical and from the driving points of view. Prost was initially slightly undervalued by the fact that he won the first nine victories of his career at the wheel of a Renault – a car it was difficult to quantify against its rivals from 1981 to '83. There was seldom such a question mark hanging over the competitive quality of Clark's Lotuses. From 1962 to 1965 and from the start of 1967 through to his death, Clark had cars which were absolutely the class of the field. Prost enjoyed that luxury only in 1984, in the McLaren-TAG's heyday. Alain also had to beat highly competitive team-mates in similar cars during 1981 and '82 (Arnoux), 1984 and '85 (Lauda) and 1986 (Rosberg). That's how Alain came out at the top of my list.

MAURICE HAMILTON'S
TOP TEN

1. **Stirling Moss**

2. **Juan Manuel Fangio**

3. **Alain Prost**

4. **Jim Clark**

5. **Alberto Ascari**

6. **Jackie Stewart**

7. **Niki Lauda**

8. **Gilles Villeneuve**

9. **Mario Andretti**

10. **Ronnie Peterson**

Remember, it's only a sport! And this is a wonderful indulgence complicated by the fact that three of the drivers were but fleeting images in my childhood. I have had to rely on the printed word and the opinions of others. But, in a way, that's true of drivers I have seen and worked with on a professional basis. How on earth can a mere mortal standing on the trackside make a valued judgement about drivers doing remarkable things with racing cars? The diffuse nature of Grand Prix racing these days makes that even more difficult. But it's not impossible.

Stirling Moss is Number One simply because of his brilliance in whatever form of racing he turned his hand to. Fangio may have been the master in Grand Prix racing but Moss, all round, had the edge.

The shame is that we did not see Jim Clark racing against the depth and quality of opposition faced on a more regular basis by Alain Prost. And there's the thought that Clark's cars were usually vastly superior to anything else. Yet Clark was astonishing in a Lotus Cortina – a far cry from a Formula 1 car, maybe, but it gave a thrilling indication of a supreme natural. My only wish is that today's Grand Prix drivers were allowed to relax and exercise their talents in other forms of motor racing. After all, it's only a sport . . .

1950 CHAMPION: **GIUSEPPE FARINA**

BRITISH GP	Silverstone	GIUSEPPE FARINA	Alfa Romeo
MONACO GP	Monte Carlo	JUAN-MANUEL FANGIO	Alfa Romeo
SWISS GP	Bremgarten	GIUSEPPE FARINA	Alfa Romeo
BELGIAN GP	Spa	JUAN-MANUEL FANGIO	Alfa Romeo
FRENCH GP	Reims	JUAN-MANUEL FANGIO	Alfa Romeo
ITALIAN GP	Monza	GIUSEPPE FARINA	Alfa Romeo

1951 CHAMPION: **JUAN-MANUEL FANGIO**

SWISS GP	Bremgarten	JUAN-MANUEL FANGIO	Alfa Romeo
BELGIAN GP	Spa	GIUSEPPE FARINA	Alfa Romeo
FRENCH GP	Reims	JUAN-MANUEL FANGIO/ LUIGI FAGIOLI	Alfa Romeo
BRITISH GP	Silverstone	FROILAN GONZALEZ	Ferrari
GERMAN GP	Nürburgring	ALBERTO ASCARI	Ferrari
ITALIAN GP	Monza	ALBERTO ASCARI	Ferrari
SPANISH GP	Pedralbes	JUAN-MANUEL FANGIO	Alfa Romeo

1952 CHAMPION: **ALBERTO ASCARI**

SWISS GP	Bremgarten	PIERO TARUFFI	Ferrari
BELGIAN GP	Spa	ALBERTO ASCARI	Ferrari
FRENCH GP	Rouen	ALBERTO ASCARI	Ferrari
BRITISH GP	Silverstone	ALBERTO ASCARI	Ferrari
GERMAN GP	Nürburgring	ALBERTO ASCARI	Ferrari
DUTCH GP	Zandvoort	ALBERTO ASCARI	Ferrari
ITALIAN GP	Monza	ALBERTO ASCARI	Ferrari

1953 CHAMPION: **ALBERTO ASCARI**

ARGENTINE GP	Buenos Aires	ALBERTO ASCARI	Ferrari
DUTCH GP	Zandvoort	ALBERTO ASCARI	Ferrari
BELGIAN GP	Spa	ALBERTO ASCARI	Ferrari
FRENCH GP	Reims	MIKE HAWTHORN	Ferrari
BRITISH GP	Silverstone	ALBERTO ASCARI	Ferrari
GERMAN GP	Nürburgring	GIUSEPPE FARINA	Ferrari
SWISS GP	Bremgarten	ALBERTO ASCARI	Ferrari
ITALIAN GP	Monza	JUAN-MANUEL FANGIO	Maserati

1954 CHAMPION: **JUAN-MANUEL FANGIO**

ARGENTINE GP	Buenos Aires	JUAN-MANUEL FANGIO	Maserati
BELGIAN GP	Spa	JUAN-MANUEL FANGIO	Maserati
FRENCH GP	Reims	JUAN-MANUEL FANGIO	Mercedes-Benz
BRITISH GP	Silverstone	FROILAN GONZALEZ	Ferrari
GERMAN GP	Nürburgring	JUAN-MANUEL FANGIO	Mercedes-Benz
SWISS GP	Bremgarten	JUAN-MANUEL FANGIO	Mercedes-Benz
ITALIAN GP	Monza	JUAN-MANUEL FANGIO	Mercedes-Benz
SPANISH GP	Pedralbes	MIKE HAWTHORN	Ferrari

1955 CHAMPION: **JUAN-MANUEL FANGIO**

ARGENTINE GP	Buenos Aires	JUAN-MANUEL FANGIO	Mercedes-Benz
MONACO GP	Monte Carlo	MAURICE TRINTIGNANT	Ferrari
BELGIAN GP	Spa	JUAN-MANUEL FANGIO	Mercedes-Benz
DUTCH GP	Zandvoort	JUAN-MANUEL FANGIO	Mercedes-Benz
BRITISH GP	Aintree	STIRLING MOSS	Mercedes-Benz
ITALIAN GP	Monza	JUAN-MANUEL FANGIO	Mercedes-Benz

1956 CHAMPION: **JUAN-MANUEL FANGIO**

ARGENTINE GP	Buenos Aires	JUAN-MANUEL FANGIO/ LUIGI MUSSO	Ferrari
MONACO GP	Monte Carlo	STIRLING MOSS	Maserati
BELGIAN GP	Spa	PETER COLLINS	Ferrari
FRENCH GP	Reims	PETER COLLINS	Ferrari
BRITISH GP	Silverstone	JUAN-MANUEL FANGIO	Ferrari
GERMAN GP	Nürburgring	JUAN-MANUEL FANGIO	Ferrari
ITALIAN GP	Monza	STIRLING MOSS	Maserati

1957 CHAMPION: **JUAN-MANUEL FANGIO**

ARGENTINE GP	Buenos Aires	JUAN-MANUEL FANGIO	Maserati
MONACO GP	Monte Carlo	JUAN-MANUEL FANGIO	Maserati
FRENCH GP	Rouen	JUAN-MANUEL FANGIO	Maserati
BRITISH GP	Aintree	STIRLING MOSS/ TONY BROOKS	Vanwall
GERMAN GP	Nürburgring	JUAN-MANUEL FANGIO	Maserati
PESCARA GP	Pescara	STIRLING MOSS	Vanwall
ITALIAN GP	Monza	STIRLING MOSS	Vanwall

1958 CHAMPION: **MIKE HAWTHORN**

ARGENTINE GP	Buenos Aires	STIRLING MOSS	Cooper
MONACO GP	Monte Carlo	MAURICE TRINTIGNANT	Cooper
DUTCH GP	Zandvoort	STIRLING MOSS	Vanwall
BELGIAN GP	Spa	TONY BROOKS	Vanwall
FRENCH GP	Reims	MIKE HAWTHORN	Ferrari
BRITISH GP	Silverstone	PETER COLLINS	Ferrari
GERMAN GP	Nürburgring	TONY BROOKS	Vanwall
PORTUGUESE GP	Oporto	STIRLING MOSS	Vanwall
ITALIAN GP	Monza	TONY BROOKS	Vanwall
MOROCCAN GP	Casablanca	STIRLING MOSS	Vanwall

1959 CHAMPION: **JACK BRABHAM**

MONACO GP	Monte Carlo	JACK BRABHAM	Cooper
DUTCH GP	Zandvoort	JOAKIM BONNIER	BRM
FRENCH GP	Reims	TONY BROOKS	Ferrari
BRITISH GP	Aintree	JACK BRABHAM	Cooper
GERMAN GP	Avus Circuit	TONY BROOKS	Ferrari
PORTUGUESE GP	Monsanto	STIRLING MOSS	Cooper
ITALIAN GP	Monza	STIRLING MOSS	Cooper
U.S. GP	Sebring	BRUCE McLAREN	Cooper

1960 CHAMPION: **JACK BRABHAM**

ARGENTINE GP	Buenos Aires	BRUCE McLAREN	Cooper
MONACO GP	Monte Carlo	STIRLING MOSS	Lotus
DUTCH GP	Zandvoort	JACK BRABHAM	Cooper
BELGIAN GP	Spa	JACK BRABHAM	Cooper
FRENCH GP	Reims	JACK BRABHAM	Cooper
BRITISH GP	Silverstone	JACK BRABHAM	Cooper
PORTUGUESE GP	Oporto	JACK BRABHAM	Cooper
ITALIAN GP	Monza	PHIL HILL	Ferrari
U.S. GP	Riverside	STIRLING MOSS	Lotus

1961 CHAMPION: **PHIL HILL**

MONACO GP	Monte Carlo	STIRLING MOSS	Lotus
DUTCH GP	Zandvoort	WOLFGANG VON TRIPS	Ferrari
BELGIAN GP	Spa	PHIL HILL	Ferrari
FRENCH GP	Reims	GIANCARLO BAGHETTI	Ferrari
BRITISH GP	Aintree	WOLFGANG VON TRIPS	Ferrari
GERMAN GP	Nürburgring	STIRLING MOSS	Lotus
ITALIAN GP	Monza	PHIL HILL	Ferrari
U.S. GP	Watkins Glen	INNES IRELAND	Lotus

1962 CHAMPION: **GRAHAM HILL**

DUTCH GP	Zandvoort	GRAHAM HILL	BRM
MONACO GP	Monte Carlo	BRUCE McLAREN	Cooper
BELGIAN GP	Spa	JIM CLARK	Lotus
FRENCH GP	Rouen	DAN GURNEY	Porsche
BRITISH GP	Aintree	JIM CLARK	Lotus
GERMAN GP	Nürburgring	GRAHAM HILL	BRM
ITALIAN GP	Monza	GRAHAM HILL	BRM
U.S. GP	Watkins Glen	JIM CLARK	Lotus
SOUTH AFRICAN GP	East London	GRAHAM HILL	BRM

1963 CHAMPION: **JIM CLARK**

MONACO GP	Monte Carlo	GRAHAM HILL	BRM
BELGIAN GP	Spa	JIM CLARK	Lotus
DUTCH GP	Zandvoort	JIM CLARK	Lotus
FRENCH GP	Reims	JIM CLARK	Lotus
BRITISH GP	Silverstone	JIM CLARK	Lotus
GERMAN GP	Nürburgring	JOHN SURTEES	Ferrari
ITALIAN GP	Monza	JIM CLARK	Lotus
U.S. GP	Watkins Glen	GRAHAM HILL	BRM
MEXICAN GP	Mexico City	JIM CLARK	Lotus
SOUTH AFRICAN GP	East London	JIM CLARK	Lotus

1964 CHAMPION: **JOHN SURTEES**

MONACO GP	Monte Carlo	GRAHAM HILL	BRM
DUTCH GP	Zandvoort	JIM CLARK	Lotus
BELGIAN GP	Spa	JIM CLARK	Lotus
FRENCH GP	Rouen	DAN GURNEY	Brabham
BRITISH GP	Brands Hatch	JIM CLARK	Lotus
GERMAN GP	Nürburgring	JOHN SURTEES	Ferrari
AUSTRIAN GP	Zeltweg	LORENZO BANDINI	Ferrari
ITALIAN GP	Monza	JOHN SURTEES	Ferrari
U.S. GP	Watkins Glen	GRAHAM HILL	BRM
MEXICAN GP	Mexico City	DAN GURNEY	Brabham

1965 CHAMPION: **JIM CLARK**

SOUTH AFRICAN GP	East London	JIM CLARK	Lotus
MONACO GP	Monte Carlo	GRAHAM HILL	BRM
BELGIAN GP	Spa	JIM CLARK	Lotus
FRENCH GP	Clermont Ferrand	JIM CLARK	Lotus
BRITISH GP	Silverstone	JIM CLARK	Lotus
DUTCH GP	Zandvoort	JIM CLARK	Lotus
GERMAN GP	Nürburgring	JIM CLARK	Lotus
ITALIAN GP	Monza	JACKIE STEWART	BRM
U.S. GP	Watkins Glen	GRAHAM HILL	BRM
MEXICAN GP	Mexico City	RICHIE GINTHER	Honda

1966 CHAMPION: **JACK BRABHAM**

MONACO GP	Monte Carlo	JACKIE STEWART	BRM
BELGIAN GP	Spa	JOHN SURTEES	Ferrari
FRENCH GP	Reims	JACK BRABHAM	Brabham
BRITISH GP	Brands Hatch	JACK BRABHAM	Brabham
DUTCH GP	Zandvoort	JACK BRABHAM	Brabham
GERMAN GP	Nürburgring	JACK BRABHAM	Brabham
ITALIAN GP	Monza	LUDOVICO SCARFIOTTI	Ferrari
U.S. GP	Watkins Glen	JIM CLARK	Lotus
MEXICAN GP	Mexico City	JOHN SURTEES	Cooper

1967 CHAMPION: **DENNY HULME**

SOUTH AFRICAN GP	Kyalami	PEDRO RODRIGUEZ	Cooper
MONACO GP	Monte Carlo	DENNY HULME	Brabham
DUTCH GP	Zandvoort	JIM CLARK	Lotus
BELGIAN GP	Spa	DAN GURNEY	Eagle
FRENCH GP	Le Mans	JACK BRABHAM	Brabham
BRITISH GP	Silverstone	JIM CLARK	Lotus
GERMAN GP	Nürburgring	DENNY HULME	Brabham
CANADIAN GP	Mosport	JACK BRABHAM	Brabham
ITALIAN GP	Monza	JOHN SURTEES	Honda
U.S. GP	Watkins Glen	JIM CLARK	Lotus
MEXICAN GP	Mexico City	JIM CLARK	Lotus

1968 CHAMPION: **GRAHAM HILL**

SOUTH AFRICAN GP	Kyalami	JIM CLARK	Lotus
SPANISH GP	Járama	GRAHAM HILL	Lotus
MONACO GP	Monte Carlo	GRAHAM HILL	Lotus
BELGIAN GP	Spa	BRUCE McLAREN	McLaren
DUTCH GP	Zandvoort	JACKIE STEWART	Matra
FRENCH GP	Rouen	JACKY ICKX	Ferrari
BRITISH GP	Brands Hatch	JO SIFFERT	Lotus
GERMAN GP	Nürburgring	JACKIE STEWART	Matra
ITALIAN GP	Monza	DENNY HULME	McLaren
CANADIAN GP	Mont-Tremblant	DENNY HULME	McLaren
U.S. GP	Watkins Glen	JACKIE STEWART	Matra
MEXICAN GP	Mexico City	GRAHAM HILL	Lotus

1969 CHAMPION: **JACKIE STEWART**

SOUTH AFRICAN GP	Kyalami	JACKIE STEWART	Matra
SPANISH GP	Montjuich	JACKIE STEWART	Matra
MONACO GP	Monte Carlo	GRAHAM HILL	Lotus
DUTCH GP	Zandvoort	JACKIE STEWART	Matra
FRENCH GP	Clermont Ferrand	JACKIE STEWART	Matra
BRITISH GP	Silverstone	JACKIE STEWART	Matra
GERMAN GP	Nürburgring	JACKY ICKX	Brabham
ITALIAN GP	Monza	JACKIE STEWART	Matra
CANADIAN GP	Mosport	JACKY ICKX	Brabham
U.S. GP	Watkins Glen	JOCHEN RINDT	Lotus
MEXICAN GP	Mexico City	DENNY HULME	McLaren

1970 CHAMPION: **JOCHEN RINDT**

SOUTH AFRICAN GP	Kyalami	JACK BRABHAM	Brabham
SPANISH GP	Járama	JACKIE STEWART	March
MONACO GP	Monte Carlo	JOCHEN RINDT	Lotus
BELGIAN GP	Spa	PEDRO RODRIGUEZ	BRM
DUTCH GP	Zandvoort	JOCHEN RINDT	Lotus
FRENCH GP	Clermont Ferrand	JOCHEN RINDT	Lotus
BRITISH GP	Brands Hatch	JOCHEN RINDT	Lotus
GERMAN GP	Hockenheim	JOCHEN RINDT	Lotus
AUSTRIAN GP	Österreichring	JACKY ICKX	Ferrari
ITALIAN GP	Monza	CLAY REGAZZONI	Ferrari
CANADIAN GP	Mont-Tremblant	JACKY ICKX	Ferrari
U.S. GP	Watkins Glen	EMERSON FITTIPALDI	Lotus
MEXICAN GP	Mexico City	JACKY ICKX	Ferrari

1971 CHAMPION: **JACKIE STEWART**

SOUTH AFRICAN GP	Kyalami	MARIO ANDRETTI	Ferrari
SPANISH GP	Montjuich	JACKIE STEWART	Tyrrell
MONACO GP	Monte Carlo	JACKIE STEWART	Tyrrell
DUTCH GP	Zandvoort	JACKY ICKX	Ferrari
FRENCH GP	Le Castellet	JACKIE STEWART	Tyrrell
BRITISH GP	Silverstone	JACKIE STEWART	Tyrrell
GERMAN GP	Nürburgring	JACKIE STEWART	Tyrrell
AUSTRIAN GP	Österreichring	JO SIFFERT	BRM
ITALIAN GP	Monza	PETER GETHIN	BRM
CANADIAN GP	Mosport	JACKIE STEWART	Tyrrell
U.S. GP	Watkins Glen	FRANÇOIS CEVERT	Tyrrell

1972 CHAMPION: **EMERSON FITTIPALDI**

ARGENTINE GP	Buenos Aires	JACKIE STEWART	Tyrrell
SOUTH AFRICAN GP	Kyalami	DENNY HULME	McLaren
SPANISH GP	Járama	EMERSON FITTIPALDI	Lotus
MONACO GP	Monte Carlo	JEAN-PIERRE BELTOISE	BRM
BELGIAN GP	Nivelles	EMERSON FITTIPALDI	Lotus
FRENCH GP	Clermont Ferrand	JACKIE STEWART	Tyrrell
BRITISH GP	Brands Hatch	EMERSON FITTIPALDI	Lotus
GERMAN GP	Nürburgring	JACKY ICKX	Ferrari
AUSTRIAN GP	Österreichring	EMERSON FITTIPALDI	Lotus
ITALIAN GP	Monza	EMERSON FITTIPALDI	Lotus
CANADIAN GP	Mosport	JACKIE STEWART	Tyrrell
U.S. GP	Watkins Glen	JACKIE STEWART	Tyrrell

1973 CHAMPION: **JACKIE STEWART**

ARGENTINE GP	Buenos Aires	EMERSON FITTIPALDI	Lotus
BRAZILIAN GP	Interlagos	EMERSON FITTPALDI	Lotus
SOUTH AFRICAN GP	Kyalami	JACKIE STEWART	Tyrrell
SPANISH GP	Montjuich	EMERSON FITTIPALDI	Lotus
BELGIAN GP	Zolder	JACKIE STEWART	Tyrrell
MONACO GP	Monte Carlo	JACKIE STEWART	Tyrrell
SWEDISH GP	Anderstorp	DENNY HULME	McLaren
FRENCH GP	Le Castellet	RONNIE PETERSON	Lotus
BRITISH GP	Silverstone	PETER REVSON	McLaren
DUTCH GP	Zandvoort	JACKIE STEWART	Tyrrell
GERMAN GP	Nürburgring	JACKIE STEWART	Tyrrell
AUSTRIAN GP	Österreichring	RONNIE PETERSON	Lotus
ITALIAN GP	Monza	RONNIE PETERSON	Lotus
CANADIAN GP	Mosport	PETER REVSON	McLaren
U.S. GP	Watkins Glen	RONNIE PETERSON	Lotus

1974 CHAMPION: **EMERSON FITTIPALDI**

GP	Circuit	Winner	Team
ARGENTINE GP	Buenos Aires	DENNY HULME	McLaren
BRAZILIAN GP	Interlagos	EMERSON FITTIPALDI	McLaren
SOUTH AFRICAN GP	Kyalami	CARLOS REUTEMANN	Brabham
SPANISH GP	Járama	NIKI LAUDA	Ferrari
BELGIAN GP	Nivelles	EMERSON FITTPALDI	McLaren
MONACO GP	Monte Carlo	RONNIE PETERSON	Lotus
SWEDISH GP	Anderstorp	JODY SCHECKTER	Tyrrell
DUTCH GP	Zandvoort	NIKI LAUDA	Ferrari
FRENCH GP	Dijon-Prenois	RONNIE PETERSON	Lotus
BRITISH GP	Brands Hatch	JODY SCHECKTER	Tyrrell
GERMAN GP	Nürburgring	CLAY REGAZZONI	Ferrari
AUSTRIAN GP	Österreichring	CARLOS REUTEMANN	Brabham
ITALIAN GP	Monza	RONNIE PETERSON	Lotus
CANADIAN GP	Mosport	EMERSON FITTIPALDI	McLaren
U.S. GP	Watkins Glen	CARLOS REUTEMANN	Brabham

1975 CHAMPION: **NIKI LAUDA**

GP	Circuit	Winner	Team
ARGENTINE GP	Buenos Aires	EMERSON FITTIPALDI	McLaren
BRAZILIAN GP	Interlagos	CARLOS PACE	Brabham
SOUTH AFRICAN GP	Kyalami	JODY SCHECKTER	Tyrrell
SPANISH GP	Montjuich	JOCHEN MASS	McLaren
MONACO GP	Monte Carlo	NIKI LAUDA	Ferrari
BELGIAN GP	Zolder	NIKI LAUDA	Ferrari
SWEDISH GP	Anderstorp	NIKI LAUDA	Ferrari
DUTCH GP	Zandvoort	JAMES HUNT	Hesketh
FRENCH GP	Le Castellet	NIKI LAUDA	Ferrari
BRITISH GP	Silverstone	EMERSON FITTIPALDI	McLaren
GERMAN GP	Nürburgring	CARLOS REUTEMANN	Brabham
AUSTRIAN GP	Österreichring	VITTORIO BRAMBILLA	March
ITALIAN GP	Monza	CLAY REGAZZONI	Ferrari
U.S. GP	Watkins Glen	NIKI LAUDA	Ferrari

1976 CHAMPION: **JAMES HUNT**

GP	Circuit	Winner	Team
BRAZILIAN GP	Interlagos	NIKI LAUDA	Ferrari
SOUTH AFRICAN GP	Kyalami	NIKI LAUDA	Ferrari
U.S. (WEST) GP	Long Beach	CLAY REGAZZONI	Ferrari
SPANISH GP	Járama	JAMES HUNT	McLaren
BELGIAN GP	Zolder	NIKI LAUDA	Ferrari
MONACO GP	Monte Carlo	NIKI LAUDA	Ferrari
SWEDISH GP	Anderstorp	JODY SCHECKTER	Tyrrell
FRENCH GP	Le Castellet	JAMES HUNT	McLaren
BRITISH GP	Brands Hatch	NIKI LAUDA	Ferrari
GERMAN GP	Nürburgring	JAMES HUNT	McLaren
AUSTRIAN GP	Österreichring	JOHN WATSON	Penske
DUTCH GP	Zandvoort	JAMES HUNT	McLaren
ITALIAN GP	Monza	RONNIE PETERSON	March
CANADIAN GP	Mosport	JAMES HUNT	McLaren
U.S. (EAST) GP	Watkins Glen	JAMES HUNT	McLaren
JAPANESE GP	Mount Fuji	MARIO ANDRETTI	Lotus

1977 CHAMPION: **NIKI LAUDA**

GP	Circuit	Winner	Team
ARGENTINE GP	Buenos Aires	JODY SCHECKTER	Wolf
BRAZILIAN GP	Interlagos	CARLOS REUTEMANN	Ferrari
SOUTH AFRICAN GP	Kyalami	NIKI LAUDA	Ferrari
U.S. (WEST) GP	Long Beach	MARIO ANDRETTI	Lotus
SPANISH GP	Járama	MARIO ANDRETTI	Lotus
MONACO GP	Monte Carlo	JODY SCHECKTER	Wolf
BELGIAN GP	Zolder	GUNNAR NILSSON	Lotus
SWEDISH GP	Anderstorp	JACQUES LAFFITE	Ligier
FRENCH GP	Dijon-Prenois	MARIO ANDRETTI	Lotus
BRITISH GP	Silverstone	JAMES HUNT	McLaren
GERMAN GP	Hockenheim	NIKI LAUDA	Ferrari
AUSTRIAN GP	Österreichring	ALAN JONES	Shadow
DUTCH GP	Zandvoort	NIKI LAUDA	Ferrari
ITALIAN GP	Monza	MARIO ANDRETTI	Lotus
U.S. (EAST) GP	Watkins Glen	JAMES HUNT	McLaren
CANADIAN GP	Mosport	JODY SCHECKTER	Wolf
JAPANESE GP	Mount Fuji	JAMES HUNT	McLaren

1978 CHAMPION: **MARIO ANDRETTI**

GP	Circuit	Winner	Team
ARGENTINE GP	Buenos Aires	MARIO ANDRETTI	Lotus
BRAZILIAN GP	Jacarepaguà	CARLOS REUTEMANN	Ferrari
SOUTH AFRICAN GP	Kyalami	RONNIE PETERSON	Lotus
U.S. (WEST) GP	Long Beach	CARLOS REUTEMANN	Ferrari
MONACO GP	Monte Carlo	PATRICK DEPAILLER	Tyrrell
BELGIAN GP	Zolder	MARIO ANDRETTI	Lotus
SPANISH GP	Járama	MARIO ANDRETTI	Lotus
SWEDISH GP	Anderstorp	NIKI LAUDA	Brabham
FRENCH GP	Le Castellet	MARIO ANDRETTI	Lotus
BRITISH GP	Brands Hatch	CARLOS REUTEMANN	Ferrari
GERMAN GP	Hockenheim	MARIO ANDRETTI	Lotus
AUSTRIAN GP	Österreichring	RONNIE PETERSON	Lotus
DUTCH GP	Zandvoort	MARIO ANDRETTI	Lotus
ITALIAN GP	Monza	NIKI LAUDA	Brabham
U.S. (EAST) GP	Watkins Glen	CARLOS REUTEMANN	Ferrari
CANADIAN GP	Montreal	GILLES VILLENEUVE	Ferrari

1979 CHAMPION: **JODY SCHECKTER**

GP	Circuit	Winner	Team
ARGENTINE GP	Buenos Aires	JACQUES LAFFITE	Ligier
BRAZILIAN GP	Interlagos	JACQUES LAFFITE	Ligier
SOUTH AFRICAN GP	Kyalami	GILLES VILLENEUVE	Ferrari
U.S. (WEST) GP	Long Beach	GILLES VILLENEUVE	Ferrari
SPANISH GP	Járama	PATRICK DEPAILLER	Ligier
BELGIAN GP	Zolder	JODY SCHECKTER	Ferrari
MONACO GP	Monte Carlo	JODY SCHECKTER	Ferrari
FRENCH GP	Dijon-Prenois	JEAN-PIERRE JABOUILLE	Renault
BRITISH GP	Silverstone	CLAY REGAZZONI	Williams
GERMAN GP	Hockenheim	ALAN JONES	Williams
AUSTRIAN GP	Österreichring	ALAN JONES	Williams
DUTCH GP	Zandvoort	ALAN JONES	Williams
ITALIAN GP	Monza	JODY SCHECKTER	Ferrari
CANADIAN GP	Montreal	ALAN JONES	Williams
U.S. GP	Watkins Glen	GILLES VILLENEUVE	Ferrari

1980 CHAMPION: **ALAN JONES**

GP	Circuit	Winner	Team
ARGENTINE GP	Buenos Aires	ALAN JONES	Williams
BRAZILIAN GP	Interlagos	RENÉ ARNOUX	Renault
SOUTH AFRICAN GP	Kyalami	RENÉ ARNOUX	Renault
U.S. (WEST) GP	Long Beach	NELSON PIQUET	Brabham
BELGIAN GP	Zolder	DIDIER PIRONI	Ligier
MONACO GP	Monte Carlo	CARLOS REUTEMANN	Williams
FRENCH GP	Le Castellet	ALAN JONES	Williams
BRITISH GP	Brands Hatch	ALAN JONES	Williams
GERMAN GP	Hockenheim	JACQUES LAFFITE	Ligier
AUSTRIAN GP	Österreichring	JEAN-PIERRE JABOUILLE	Renault
DUTCH GP	Zandvoort	NELSON PIQUET	Brabham
ITALIAN GP	Imola	NELSON PIQUET	Brabham
CANADIAN GP	Montreal	ALAN JONES	Williams
U.S. (EAST) GP	Watkins Glen	ALAN JONES	Williams

1981 CHAMPION: **NELSON PIQUET**

GP	Circuit	Winner	Team
U.S. (WEST) GP	Long Beach	ALAN JONES	Williams
BRAZILIAN GP	Jacarepaguà	CARLOS REUTEMANN	Williams
ARGENTINE GP	Buenos Aires	NELSON PIQUET	Brabham
SAN MARINO GP	Imola	NELSON PIQUET	Brabham
BELGIAN GP	Zolder	CARLOS REUTEMANN	Williams
MONACO GP	Monte Carlo	GILLES VILLENEUVE	Ferrari
SPANISH GP	Járama	GILLES VILLENEUVE	Ferrari
FRENCH GP	Dijon-Prenois	ALAIN PROST	Renault
BRITISH GP	Silverstone	JOHN WATSON	McLaren
GERMAN GP	Hockenheim	NELSON PIQUET	Brabham
AUSTRIAN GP	Österreichring	JACQUES LAFFITE	Ligier
DUTCH GP	Zandvoort	ALAIN PROST	Renault
ITALIAN GP	Monza	ALAIN PROST	Renault
CANADIAN GP	Montreal	JACQUES LAFFITE	Ligier
U.S. GP	Las Vegas	ALAN JONES	Williams

1982 CHAMPION: **KEKE ROSBERG**

SOUTH AFRICAN GP	Kyalami	ALAIN PROST	Renault
BRAZILIAN GP	Jacarepaguà	ALAIN PROST	Renault
U.S. (WEST) GP	Long Beach	NIKI LAUDA	McLaren
SAN MARINO GP	Imola	DIDIER PIRONI	Ferrari
BELGIAN GP	Zolder	JOHN WATSON	McLaren
MONACO GP	Monte Carlo	RICCARDO PATRESE	Brabham
U.S. (EAST) GP	Detroit	JOHN WATSON	McLaren
CANADIAN GP	Montreal	NELSON PIQUET	Brabham
DUTCH GP	Zandvoort	DIDIER PIRONI	Ferrari
BRITISH GP	Brands Hatch	NIKI LAUDA	McLaren
FRENCH GP	Le Castellet	RENÉ ARNOUX	Renault
GERMAN GP	Hockenheim	PATRICK TAMBAY	Ferrari
AUSTRIAN GP	Österreichring	ELIO DE ANGELIS	Lotus
SWISS GP	Dijon-Prenois	KEKE ROSBERG	Williams
ITALIAN GP	Monza	RENÉ ARNOUX	Renault
U.S. GP	Las Vegas	MICHELE ALBORETO	Tyrrell

1983 CHAMPION: **NELSON PIQUET**

BRAZILIAN GP	Jacarepaguà	NELSON PIQUET	Brabham
U.S. (WEST) GP	Long Beach	JOHN WATSON	McLaren
FRENCH GP	Le Castellet	ALAIN PROST	Renault
SAN MARINO GP	Imola	PATRICK TAMBAY	Ferrari
MONACO GP	Monte Carlo	KEKE ROSBERG	Williams
BELGIAN GP	Spa	ALAIN PROST	Renault
U.S. (EAST) GP	Detroit	MICHELE ALBORETO	Tyrrell
CANADIAN GP	Montreal	RENÉ ARNOUX	Ferrari
BRITISH GP	Silverstone	ALAIN PROST	Renault
GERMAN GP	Hockenheim	RENÉ ARNOUX	Ferrari
AUSTRIAN GP	Österreichring	ALAIN PROST	Renault
DUTCH GP	Zandvoort	RENÉ ARNOUX	Ferrari
ITALIAN GP	Monza	NELSON PIQUET	Brabham
EUROPEAN GP	Brands Hatch	NELSON PIQUET	Brabham
SOUTH AFRICAN GP	Kyalami	RICCARDO PATRESE	Brabham

1984 CHAMPION: **NIKI LAUDA**

BRAZILIAN GP	Jacarepaguà	ALAIN PROST	McLaren
SOUTH AFRICAN GP	Kyalami	NIKI LAUDA	McLaren
BELGIAN GP	Zolder	MICHELE ALBORETO	Ferrari
SAN MARINO GP	Imola	ALAIN PROST	McLaren
FRENCH GP	Dijon-Prenois	NIKI LAUDA	McLaren
MONACO GP	Monte Carlo	ALAIN PROST	McLaren
CANADIAN GP	Montreal	NELSON PIQUET	Brabham
U.S. (EAST) GP	Detroit	NELSON PIQUET	Brabham
U.S. GP	Dallas	KEKE ROSBERG	Williams
BRITISH GP	Brands Hatch	NIKI LAUDA	McLaren
GERMAN GP	Hockenheim	ALAIN PROST	McLaren
AUSTRIAN GP	Österreichring	NIKI LAUDA	McLaren
DUTCH GP	Zandvoort	ALAIN PROST	McLaren
ITALIAN GP	Monza	NIKI LAUDA	McLaren
EUROPEAN GP	Nürburgring	ALAIN PROST	McLaren
PORTUGUESE GP	Estoril	ALAIN PROST	McLaren

1985 CHAMPION: **ALAIN PROST**

BRAZILIAN GP	Jacarepaguà	ALAIN PROST	McLaren
PORTUGUESE GP	Estoril	AYRTON SENNA	Lotus
SAN MARINO GP	Imola	ELIO DE ANGELIS	Lotus
MONACO GP	Monte Carlo	ALAIN PROST	McLaren
CANADIAN GP	Montreal	MICHELE ALBORETO	Ferrari
U.S. GP	Detroit	KEKE ROSBERG	Williams
FRENCH GP	Le Castellet	NELSON PIQUET	Brabham
BRITISH GP	Silverstone	ALAIN PROST	McLaren
GERMAN GP	Nürburgring	MICHELE ALBORETO	Ferrari
AUSTRIAN GP	Österreichring	ALAIN PROST	McLaren
DUTCH GP	Zandvoort	NIKI LAUDA	McLaren
ITALIAN GP	Monza	ALAIN PROST	McLaren
BELGIAN GP	Spa	AYRTON SENNA	Lotus
EUROPEAN GP	Brands Hatch	NIGEL MANSELL	Williams
SOUTH AFRICAN GP	Kyalami	NIGEL MANSELL	Williams
AUSTRALIAN GP	Adelaide	KEKE ROSBERG	Williams

1986 CHAMPION: **ALAIN PROST**

BRAZILIAN GP	Rio de Janeiro	NELSON PIQUET	Williams
SPANISH GP	Jerez	AYRTON SENNA	Lotus
SAN MARINO GP	Imola	ALAIN PROST	McLaren
MONACO GP	Monte Carlo	ALAIN PROST	McLaren
BELGIAN GP	Spa	NIGEL MANSELL	Williams
CANADIAN GP	Montreal	NIGEL MANSELL	Williams
U.S. GP	Detroit	AYRTON SENNA	Lotus
FRENCH GP	Le Castellet	NIGEL MANSELL	Williams
BRITISH GP	Brands Hatch	NIGEL MANSELL	Williams
GERMAN GP	Hockenheim	NELSON PIQUET	Williams
HUNGARIAN GP	Budapest	NELSON PIQUET	Williams
AUSTRIAN GP	Österreichring	ALAIN PROST	McLaren
ITALIAN GP	Monza	NELSON PIQUET	Williams
PORTUGUESE GP	Estoril	NIGEL MANSELL	Williams
MEXICAN GP	Mexico City	GERHARD BERGER	Benetton
AUSTRALIAN GP	Adelaide	ALAIN PROST	McLaren

1987 *Results at time of going to press.*

BRAZILIAN GP	Rio de Janeiro	ALAIN PROST	McLaren
SAN MARINO GP	Imola	NIGEL MANSELL	Williams
BELGIAN GP	Spa	ALAIN PROST	McLaren
MONACO GP	Monte Carlo	AYRTON SENNA	Lotus
U.S. GP	Detroit	AYRTON SENNA	Lotus
FRENCH GP	Le Castellet	NIGEL MANSELL	Williams
BRITISH GP	Silverstone	NIGEL MANSELL	Williams

WINNERS' STATISTICS

	Wins	2nd	3rd	Pole positions	Fastest laps	GP starts	Points
MICHELE ALBORETO (ITA) b. 1956	5	7	6	2	3	96	140½
MARIO ANDRETTI (US) b. 1940	12	2	5	18	10	128	180
ELIO DE ANGELIS (ITA) 1958-1986	2	2	5	3	–	108	122
RENÉ ARNOUX (FRA) b. 1948	7	9	6	18	12	117	179
ALBERTO ASCARI (ITA) 1918–1955	13	4	–	14	11	32	139
GIANCARLO BAGHETTI (ITA) b. 1934	1	–	–	–	1	21	14
LORENZO BANDINI (ITA) 1935-1967	1	2	5	1	2	42	58
JEAN-PIERRE BELTOISE (FR) b.1937	1	3	4	–	4	85	77
GERHARD BERGER (AUT) b. 1959	1	–	1	–	1	43	33
JOAKIM BONNIER (SWE) 1930-1972	1	–	–	1	–	102	39
JACK BRABHAM (AUS) b. 1926	14	10	8	13	10	126	261
VITTORIO BRAMBILLA (ITA) b. 1937	1	–	–	1	2	74	15½
TONY BROOKS (GB) b. 1932	6	2	2	3	3	38	75
FRANÇOIS CEVERT (FRA) 1944-1973	1	10	2	–	2	46	89
JIM CLARK (GB) 1936-1968	25	1	6	33	27	72	274
PETER COLLINS (GB) 1931-1958	3	3	3	1	–	32	47
PATRICK DEPAILLER (FRA) 1944-1980	2	10	7	1	4	93	141
JUAN-MANUEL FANGIO (ARG) b. 1911	24	11	1	28	23	51	277½
GIUSEPPE FARINA (ITA) 1906-1966	5	9	6	5	6	33	128⅓
EMERSON FITTIPALDI (BRA) b. 1946	14	13	8	6	6	144	281
PETER GETHIN (GB) b. 1940	1	–	–	–	–	30	11
RICHIE GINTHER (US) b. 1930	1	8	5	–	3	52	107
FROILAN GONZALEZ (ARG) b. 1922	1	7	6	3	6	26	77½
DAN GURNEY (US) b. 1931	4	8	7	3	7	86	133
MIKE HAWTHORN (GB) 1929-1959	3	9	6	4	6	45	127½
GRAHAM HILL (GB) 1929-1975	14	15	7	13	10	176	289
PHIL HILL (US) b. 1927	3	6	7	6	6	48	98
DENNY HULME (NZ) b. 1936	8	9	17	1	9	112	248
JAMES HUNT (GB) b. 1947	10	6	7	14	8	92	179
JACKY ICKX (BEL) b. 1945	8	7	10	13	14	116	181
INNES IRELAND (GB) b. 1930	1	2	1	–	1	50	47
JEAN-PIERRE JABOUILLE (FRA) b. 1942	2	–	–	6	–	49	21
ALAN JONES (AUS) b. 1946	12	7	5	6	13	116	206
JACQUES LAFFITE (FRA) b. 1943	6	9	16	7	7	175	228
NIKI LAUDA (AUT) b. 1949	25	20	9	24	25	171	420½
NIGEL MANSELL (GB) b. 1954	10	3	7	9	8	97	169
JOCHEN MASS (GER) b. 1946	1	1	6	–	2	105	71
BRUCE McLAREN (NZ) 1937-1970	4	11	12	–	3	101	198½
STIRLING MOSS (GB) b. 1929	16	5	2	16	20	66	186½
GUNNAR NILSSON (SWE) 1948-1978	1	–	3	–	–	31	31
CARLOS PACE (BRA) 1944-1977	1	3	2	1	5	72	58
RICCARDO PATRESE (ITA) b. 1954	2	4	4	2	2	151	75
RONNIE PETERSON (SWE) 1944-1978	10	10	6	14	9	123	206
NELSON PIQUET (BRA) b. 1952	17	17	10	21	22	132	335
DIDIER PIRONI (FRA) b. 1952	3	3	7	4	6	70	101
ALAIN PROST (FRA) b. 1955	27	13	12	17	20	112	384½
CLAY REGAZZONI (SWI) b. 1939	5	13	10	5	15	132	212
CARLOS REUTEMANN (ARG) b. 1939	12	13	20	6	4	146	310
PETER REVSON (US) 1939-1974	2	2	4	1	–	30	61
JOCHEN RINDT (AUT) 1942-1970	6	3	4	10	3	60	109
PEDRO RODRIGUEZ (MEX) 1940-1971	2	3	2	–	1	55	71
KEKE ROSBERG (FIN) b. 1948	5	8	4	5	3	114	159½
LUDOVICO SCARFIOTTI (ITA) 1933-1968	1	–	–	–	1	10	17
JODY SCHECKTER (SA) b. 1950	10	14	9	3	6	112	255
AYRTON SENNA (BRA) b. 1960	6	7	7	16	5	53	134
JO SIFFERT (SWI) 1936-1971	2	2	2	2	4	97	68
JACKIE STEWART (GB) b. 1939	27	11	5	17	15	99	360
JOHN SURTEES (GB) b. 1934	6	10	8	8	11	111	180
PATRICK TAMBAY (FRA) b. 1949	2	4	5	5	2	114	103
PIERO TARUFFI (ITA) b. 1906	1	3	1	–	1	18	41
MAURICE TRINTIGNANT (FRA) b. 1917	2	3	5	–	1	82	72⅓
WOLFGANG VON TRIPS (GER) 1928-1961	2	2	2	1	–	27	56
GILLES VILLENEUVE (CAN) 1952-1982	6	5	2	2	7	67	107
JOHN WATSON (GB) b. 1946	5	6	9	2	5	152	169

Statistics up to and including 1987 British Grand Prix.